Being Good

'A slender but rich meditation on why human beings should choose to behave well when the possibilities for doing evil are so abundant...Highly accessible, highly rewarding.'

Kirkus Reviews

'enjoyable and extremely readable overview of philosophical ethics'

The Philosopher's Magazine

'a first-rate and accessible guide which tackles the huge, perpetual questions'

Nottingham Evening Post

'a nifty little guide to the thorny subject of ethics'

Independent on Sunday

Simon Blackburn is Professor of Philosophy at the University of Cambridge. Until 2000 he was Edna J. Koury Distinguished Professor of Philosophy at the University of North Carolina, Chapel Hill, and from 1969 to 1990 a fellow and Tutor at Pembroke College, Oxford. His books include *Spreading the Word* (1984), *Essays in Quasi-Realism* (1993), *The Oxford Dictionary of Philosophy* (1994), *Ruling Passions* (1998), *Truth* (co-edited with Keith Simmons, 1999), and the best-selling *Think* (1999). He edited the journal Mind from 1984 to 1990.

Being Good

A short introduction to ethics

SIMON BLACKBURN

OXFORD
UNIVERSITY PRESS

OXFORD

UNIVERSITY PRESS

Great Clarendon Street, Oxford OX2 6DP

Oxford University Press is a department of the University of Oxford
It furthers the University's objective of excellence in research, scholarship,
and education by publishing worldwide in

Oxford New York

Athens Auckland Bangkok Bogotá Buenos Aires
Cape Town Chennai Dar es Salaam Delhi Florence Hong Kong Istanbul
Karachi Kolkata Kuala Lumpur Madrid Melbourne Mexico City Mumbai
Nairobi Paris São Paulo Shanghai Singapore Taipei Tokyo Toronto Warsaw

with associated companies in Berlin Ibadan

Oxford is a registered trade mark of Oxford University Press
in the UK and in certain other countries

Published in the United States
by Oxford University Press Inc., New York

© Simon Blackburn 2001

Database right Oxford University Press (maker)

First published 2001

First published as an Oxford University Paperback 2002

British Library Cataloguing in Publication Data

Data available

Library of Congress Cataloging in Publication Data

Data available

ISBN 13: 978-0-19-285377-6

15

Typset by Invisible Ink
Printed in Great Britain
on acid-free paper by
Ashford Colour Press Ltd,
Gosport, Hants.

ॐ

Preface

THIS BOOK WAS initially designed for the series of Very Short Introductions published by Oxford University Press. For this reason it is shorter than *Think*, my other introductory book, to which it stands as a younger sibling. *Think* grew from a conviction that most introductions to philosophy were unnecessarily dry and off-putting; the present volume grew from a parallel conviction that most introductions to ethics failed to confront what really bothers people about the subject. What bothers them, I believe, are the many causes we have to fear that ethical claims are a kind of sham. The fear is called by names like relativism, scepticism, and nihilism. I have tried to weave the book around an exploration of them. But by the end it will be up to each reader to decide whether they have been laid to rest, or whether, if like Dracula they rise again, they are at least de-fanged.

I was invited to write the book by the editor of the series, Shelley Cox, whose confidence and encouragement have been towers of strength to me. The actual writing was done during the summer of 2000 at the Research School of Social Sciences of the Australian National University, perhaps the most agreeable place in the world to embark on such a project. I owe thanks to Michael Smith for the hospitality of the School. The University of North Carolina at Chapel Hill has always given me marvellous research support, and an equally marvellous critical audience of colleagues and graduate students. Among them, I owe thanks to Adrienne Martin who read the proofs. As always, my principal debt is to my wife Angela, whose editorial and typesetting skills are not usually at the service of an author under the same roof, and so needed matching by her equally remarkable patience and cheer.

24 November 2000   SWB

Contents

Illustrations

Introduction

WE HAVE ALL LEARNED to become sensitive to the physical environment. We know that we depend upon it, that it is fragile, and that we have the power to ruin it, thereby ruining our own lives, or more probably those of our descendants. Perhaps fewer of us are sensitive to what we might call the moral or ethical environment. This is the surrounding climate of ideas about how to live. It determines what we find acceptable or unacceptable, admirable or contemptible. It determines our conception of when things are going well and when they are going badly. It determines our conception of what is due to us, and what is due from us, as we relate to others. It shapes our emotional responses, determining what is a cause of pride or shame, or anger or gratitude, or what can be forgiven and what cannot. It gives us our standards—our standards of behaviour. In the eyes of some thinkers, most famously perhaps G. W. F. Hegel (1770–1831), it shapes our very identities. Our consciousness of ourselves is largely or even essentially a consciousness of how we stand for other people. We need stories of our own value in the eyes of each other, the eyes of the world. Of course, attempts to increase that value can be badly overdone, as Paul Klee shows (below).

The workings of the ethical environment can be strangely invisible. I was once defending the practice of philosophy on a radio programme where one of the other guests was a professional survivor of the Nazi concentration camps. He asked me, fairly aggressively, what use philosophy would have been on a death march? The answer, of course, was not much—no more than literature, art, music, mathematics, or science would be useful at such a time. But consider the ethical environment that made such events possible. Hitler said, 'How lucky it is for rulers that men cannot think.' But in saying this he sounded as if he, too, was blind to the ethical climate that enabled his own ideas, and hence his power, to

1. Paul Klee, 'Two Men Meet, Each Believing the Other To Be in a Higher Position'. A comment on the servility often involved in the ambition for respect.

flourish. This climate included images of the primordial purity of a particular race and people. It was permeated by fear for the fragile nature of this purity. Like America in the post-war McCarthy era, it feared pollution from 'degenerates' outside or within. It included visions of national and racial destiny. It included ideas of apocalyptic transformation through national solidarity and military dedication to a cause. It was hospitable to the idea of the leader whose godlike vision is authoritative and unchallengeable. In turn, those ideas had roots in misapplications of Darwinism, in German Romanticism, and indeed in some aspects of Judaism and Christianity. In short, Hitler could come to power only because people *did* think—but their thinking was poisoned by an enveloping climate of ideas, many of which may not even have been conscious. For we may not be aware of our ideas. An idea in this sense is a tendency to accept routes of thought and feeling that we may not recognize in ourselves, or even be able to articulate. Yet such dispositions rule the social and political world.

There is a story about a physicist visiting his colleague Niels Bohr, and expressing surprise at finding a good-luck horseshoe hanging on the wall: 'Surely you are not superstitious?' 'Oh, no, but I am told it works whether you believe in it or not.' Horseshoes do not, but the ethical climate does.

An *ethical* climate is a different thing from a *moralistic* one. Indeed, one of the marks of an ethical climate may be hostility to moralizing, which is somehow out of place or bad form. Thinking that will itself be a something that affects the way we live our lives. So, for instance, one peculiarity of our present climate is that we care much more about our rights than about our 'good'. For previous thinkers about ethics, such as those who wrote the Upan-ishads, or Confucius, or Plato, or the founders of the Christian tradition, the central concern was the state of one's soul, meaning some personal state of justice or harmony. Such a state might in-clude resignation and renunciation, or detachment, or obedience, or knowledge, especially self-knowledge. For Plato there could be no just political order except one populated by just citizens (al-though this also allows that inner harmony or 'justice' in citizens requires a just political order—there is nothing viciously circular about this interplay).

Today we tend not to believe that; we tend to think that modern constitutional democracies are fine regardless of the private vices of those within them. We are much more nervous talking about our good: it seems moralistic, or undemocratic, or elitist. Similarly, we are nervous talking about duty. The Victorian ideal of a life de-voted to duty, or a calling, is substantially lost to us. So a greater proportion of our moral energy goes to protecting claims against each other, and that includes protecting the state of our soul as purely private, purely our own business. We see some of the work-ings of this aspect of our climate in this book.

Human beings are ethical animals. I do not mean that we natur-ally behave particularly well, nor that we are endlessly telling each other what to do. But we grade and evaluate, and compare and ad-mire, and claim and justify. We do not just 'prefer' this or that, in isolation. We prefer that our preferences are shared; we turn them into demands on each other. Events endlessly adjust our sense of responsibility, our guilt and shame and our sense of our own worth and that of others. We hope for lives whose story leaves us looking admirable; we like our weaknesses to be hidden and deniable. Drama, literature, and poetry all work out ideas of standards of behaviour and their consequences. This is overtly so in great art. But it shows itself just as unmistakably in our relentless appetite for gossip and the confession shows and the soap opera. Should Arlene tell Charlene that Rod knows that Tod kissed Darlene, although nobody has told Marlene? Is it required by loyalty to Charlene or would it be a betrayal of Darlene? Watch on.

Reflection on the ethical climate is not the private preserve of a few academic theorists in universities. After all, the satirist and cartoonist, as well as the artist and the novelist, comment upon and criticize the prevailing climate just as effectively as those who get known as philosophers. The impact of a campaigning novelist, such as Harriet Beecher Stowe, Dickens, Zola, or Solzhenitsyn, may be much greater than that of the academic theorist. A single photograph may have done more to halt the Vietnam war than all the writings of moral philosophers of the time put together (see next page).

Philosophy is certainly not alone in its engagement with the ethical climate. But its reflections contain a distinctive ambition. The ambition is to understand the springs of motivation, reason, and feeling that move us. It is to understand the networks of rules or 'norms' that sustain our lives. The ambition is often one of finding system in the apparent jumble of principles and goals that we respect, or say we do. It is an enterprise of self-knowledge. Of course, philosophers do not escape the climate, even as they reflect on it. Any story about human nature in the contemporary climate is a

2. Hung Cong ('Nick') Ut, 'Accidental Napalm Attack, 1972'.

result of human nature and the contemporary climate. But such stories may be better or worse, for all that.

Admiring the enterprise, aspiring to it, and even tolerating it, are themselves moral stances. They can themselves flourish or wither at different times, depending on how much we like what we see in the mirror. Rejecting the enterprise is natural enough, especially when things are comfortable. We all have a tendency to complacency with our own ways, like the English aristocrat on the Grand Tour: 'The Italians call it a *coltello*, the French a *couteau*, the Germans a *Messer*, but the English call it a knife, and when all is said and done, that's what it is.'

We do not like being told what to do. We want to enjoy our lives, and we want to enjoy them with a good conscience. People who disturb that equilibrium are uncomfortable, so moralists are often uninvited guests at the feast, and we have a multitude of defences against them. Analogously, some individuals can insulate themselves from a poor physical environment, for a time. They may profit by creating one. The owner can live upwind of his chemical factory, and the logger may know that the trees will not give out until after he is dead. Similarly, individuals can insulate themselves from a poor moral environment, or profit from it. Just as some trees flourish by depriving others of nutrients or light, so some people flourish by depriving others of their due. The western white male may flourish because of the inferior economic or social status of people who are not western, or white, or male. Insofar as we are like that, we will not want the lid to be lifted.

Ethics is disturbing. We are often vaguely uncomfortable when we think of such things as exploitation of the world's resources, or the way our comforts are provided by the miserable labour conditions of the third world. Sometimes, defensively, we get angry when such things are brought up. But to be entrenched in a culture, rather than merely belonging to the occasional rogue, exploitative attitudes will themselves need a story. So an ethical climate may allow talking of 'the market' as a justification for *our* high prices, and talking of 'their selfishness' and 'our rights' as a justification for anger at *their* high prices. Racists and sexists, like antebellum slave owners in America, always have to tell themselves a story that justifies their system. The ethical climate will sustain a conviction that *we* are civilized, and *they* are not, or that *we* deserve our better fortune than *them*, or that *we* are intelligent, sensitive, rational, or progressive, or scientific, or authoritative, or blessed, or alone to be trusted with freedoms and rights, while *they* are not. An ethic gone wrong is an essential preliminary to the sweat-shop or the concentration camp and the death march.

I therefore begin this book with a look at the responses we sometimes give when ethics intrudes on our lives. These are responses that in different ways constitute threats to ethics. After that, in Part II, we look at some of the problems that living throws at us, and in particular the clash between principles of justice and rights, and less forbidding notions such as happiness and freedom. Finally, in Part III we look at the question of foundations: the ultimate justification for ethics, and its connection with human knowledge and human progress.

PART ONE

Seven Threats to Ethics

THIS SECTION LOOKS AT ideas that destabilize us when we think about standards of choice and conduct. In various ways they seem to suggest that ethics is somehow impossible. They are important because they themselves can seep into the moral environment. When they do, they can change what we expect from each other and ourselves, usually for the worse. Under their influence, when we look at the big words—justice, equality, freedom, rights—we see only bids for power and clashes of power, or we see only hypocrisy, or we see only our own opinions, unworthy to be foisted onto others. Cynicism and self-consciousness paralyse us. In what follows we consider seven such threats.

1. THE DEATH OF GOD

For many people, ethics is not only tied up with religion, but is completely settled by it. Such people do not need to think too much about ethics, because there is an authoritative code of instructions, a handbook of how to live. It is the word of Heaven, or the will of a Being greater than ourselves. The standards of living become known to us by revelation of this Being. Either we take ourselves to perceive the fountainhead directly, or more often we have the benefit of an intermediary—a priest, or a prophet, or a text, or a tradition sufficiently in touch with the divine will to be able to communicate it to us. Then we know what to do. Obedience to the divine will is meritorious, and brings reward; disobedience is lethally punished. In the Christian version, obedience brings triumph over death, or everlasting life. Disobedience means eternal Hell.

In the nineteenth century, in the west, when traditional religious belief began to lose its grip, many thinkers felt that ethics went with it. It is not to the purpose here to assess whether such belief should have lost its grip. Our question is the implication for our standards of behaviour. Is it true that, as Dostoevsky said, 'If God is dead, everything is permitted'? It might seem to be true: without a lawgiver, how can there be a law?

Before thinking about this more directly, we might take a diversion through some of the shortcomings in traditional religious instruction. Anyone reading the Bible might be troubled by some of its precepts. The Old Testament God is partial to some people above others, and above all jealous of his own pre-eminence, a strange moral obsession. He seems to have no problem with a slave-owning society, believes that birth control is a capital crime (Genesis 38: 9–10), is keen on child abuse (Proverbs 22: 15, 23: 13–14, 29: 15), and, for good measure, approves of fool abuse (Proverbs 26: 3). Indeed, there is a letter going around the Internet, purporting to be written to 'Doctor Laura', a fundamentalist agony aunt:

Dear Dr Laura,

Thank you for doing so much to educate people regarding God's Law. I have learned a great deal from you, and I try to share that knowledge with as many people as I can. When someone tries to defend the homosexual lifestyle, for example, I simply remind him that Leviticus 18: 22 clearly states it to be an abomination. End of debate. I do need some advice from you, however, regarding some of the specific laws and how to best follow them.

a. When I burn a bull on the altar as a sacrifice, I know it creates a pleasing odor for the Lord (Lev. 1: 9). The problem is my neighbors. They claim the odor is not pleasing to them. How should I deal with this?

b. I would like to sell my daughter into slavery, as it suggests in Exodus 21: 7. In this day and age, what do you think would be a fair price for her?

c. I know that I am allowed no contact with a woman while she is in her period of menstrual uncleanliness (Lev. 15: 19–24). The problem is, how do I tell? I have tried asking, but most women take offense.

d. Leviticus 25: 44 states that I may buy slaves from the

nations that are around us. A friend of mine claims that this applies to Mexicans, but not Canadians. Can you clarify?

e. I have a neighbor who insists on working on the Sabbath. Exodus 35: 2 clearly states he should be put to death. Am I morally obligated to kill him myself?

f. A friend of mine feels that even though eating shellfish is an abomination (Lev. 10: 10), it is a lesser abomination than homosexuality. I don't agree. Can you settle this?

g. Leviticus 21: 20 states that I may not approach the altar of God if I have a defect in my sight. I have to admit that I wear reading glasses. Does my vision have to be 20/20, or is there some wiggle room here?

I know you have studied these things extensively, so I am confident you can help. Thank you again for reminding us that God's word is eternal and unchanging.

Things are usually supposed to get better in the New Testament, with its admirable emphasis on love, forgiveness, and meekness. Yet the overall story of 'atonement' and 'redemption' is morally dubious, suggesting as it does that justice can be satisfied by the sacrifice of an innocent for the sins of the guilty—the doctrine of the scapegoat. Then the persona of Jesus in the Gospels has his fair share of moral quirks. He can be sectarian: 'Go not into the way of the Gentiles, and into any city of the Samaritans enter ye not. But go rather to the lost sheep of the house of Israel' (Matt. 10: 5–6). In a similar vein, he refuses help to the non-Jewish woman from Canaan with the chilling racist remark, 'It is not meet to take the children's bread, and cast it to dogs' (Matt. 15: 26; Mark 7: 27). He wants us to be gentle, meek, and mild, but he himself is far from it:

'Ye serpents, ye generation of vipers, how can ye escape the damnation of hell?' (Matt. 23: 33). The episode of the Gadarene swine shows him to share the then-popular belief that mental illness is caused by possession by devils. It also shows that animal lives—also anybody else's property rights in pigs—have no value (Luke 8: 27–33). The events of the fig tree in Bethany (Mark 11: 12–21) would make any environmentalist's hair stand on end.

Finally there are sins of omission as well as sins of commission. So we might wonder as well why he is not shown explicitly countermanding some of the rough bits of the Old Testament. Exodus 22: 18, 'Thou shalt not suffer a witch to live,' helped to burn alive tens or hundreds of thousands of women in Europe and America between around 1450 and 1780. It would have been helpful to suffering humanity, one might think, had a supremely good and caring and knowledgeable person, foreseeing this, revoked the injunction.

All in all, then, the Bible can be read as giving us a carte blanche for harsh attitudes to children, the mentally handicapped, animals, the environment, the divorced, unbelievers, people with various sexual habits, and elderly women. It encourages harsh attitudes to ourselves, as fallen creatures endlessly polluted by sin, and hatred of ourselves inevitably brings hatred of others.

The philosopher who mounted the most famous and sustained attack against the moral climate fostered by Christianity was Friedrich Nietzsche (1844–1900). Here he is in full flow:

> Under Christianity the instincts of the subjugated and the oppressed come to the fore: it is only those who are at the bottom who seek their salvation in it. Here the prevailing pastime, the

favourite remedy for boredom is the discussion of sin, self-criticism, the inquisition of conscience; here the emotion produced by power (called 'God') is pumped up (by prayer); here the highest good is regarded as unattainable, as a gift, as 'grace'. Here, too, open dealing is lacking; concealment and the darkened room are Christian. Here body is despised and hygiene is denounced as sensual; the church even ranges itself against cleanliness (—the first Christian order after the banishment of the Moors closed the public baths, of which there were 270 in Cordova alone). Christian, too, is a certain cruelty toward one's self and toward others; hatred of unbelievers; the will to persecute... And Christian is all hatred of the intellect, of pride, of courage, of freedom, of intellectual libertinage; Christian is all hatred of the senses, of joy in the senses, of joy in general.

Obviously there have been, and will be, apologists who want to defend or explain away the embarrassing elements. Similarly, apologists for Hinduism defend or explain away its involvement with the caste system, and apologists for Islam defend or explain away its harsh penal code or its attitude to women and infidels. What is interesting, however, is that when we weigh up these attempts we are ourselves in the process of assessing moral standards. We are able to stand back from any text, however entrenched, far enough to ask whether it represents an admirable or acceptable morality, or whether we ought to accept some bits, but reject others. So again the question arises: where do these standards come from, if they have the authority to judge even our best religious traditions?

The classic challenge to the idea that ethics can have a religious foundation is provided by Plato (c. 429–347 BC), in the dialogue known as the *Euthyphro*. In this dialogue, Socrates, who is on the point of being tried for impiety, encounters one Euthyphro, who sets himself up as knowing exactly what piety or justice is. Indeed, so sure is he, that he is on the point of prosecuting his own father for causing a death.

> EUTH. *Yes, I should say that what all the gods love is pious and holy, and the opposite which they all hate, impious.*
>
> SOC. *Ought we to enquire into the truth of this, Euthyphro, or simply to accept the mere statement on our own authority and that of others? What do you say?*
>
> EUTH. *We should enquire; and I believe that the statement will stand the test of enquiry.*
>
> SOC. *We shall know better, my good friend, in a little while. The point which I should first wish to understand is whether the pious or holy is beloved by the gods because it is holy, or holy because it is beloved of the gods.*

Once he has posed this question, Socrates has no trouble coming down on one side of it:

> SOC. *And what do you say of piety, Euthyphro: is not piety, according to your definition, loved by all the gods?*
>
> EUTH. *Yes.*
>
> SOC. *Because it is pious or holy, or for some other reason?*
>
> EUTH. *No, that is the reason.*
>
> SOC. *It is loved because it is holy, not holy because it is loved?*
>
> EUTH. *Yes.*
>
> SOC. *And that which is dear to the gods is loved by them and is in a state to be loved of them because it is loved of them?*

EUTH. *Certainly.*

SOC. *Then that which is dear to the gods, Euthyphro, is not holy, nor is that which is holy loved of God, as you affirm; but they are two different things.*

EUTH. *How do you mean, Socrates?*

SOC. *I mean to say that the holy has been acknowledged by us to be loved of God because it is holy, not to be holy because it is loved.*

The point is that God, or the gods, are not to be thought of as *arbitrary*. They have to be regarded as selecting the *right* things to allow and to forbid. They have to latch on to what is holy or just, exactly as we do. It is not given that they do this simply because they are powerful, or created everything, or have horrendous punishments and delicious rewards in their gifts. That doesn't make them *good*. Furthermore, to obey their commandments just because of their power would be servile and self-interested. Suppose, for instance, I am minded to do something bad, such as to betray someone's trust. It isn't good enough if I think: 'Well, let me see, the gains are such-and-such, but now I have to factor in the chance of God hitting me hard if I do it. On the other hand, God is forgiving and there is a good chance I can fob him off by confession, or by a deathbed repentance later …' These are not the thoughts of a good character. The good character is supposed to think: 'It would be a betrayal, so I won't do it.' That's the end of the story. To go in for a religious cost-benefit analysis is, in a phrase made famous by the contemporary moral philosopher Bernard Williams, to have 'one thought too many'.

The detour through an external god, then, seems worse than irrelevant. It seems to distort the very idea of a standard of conduct. As the moral philosopher Immanuel Kant (1724–1804) put it, it encourages us to act in *accordance* with a rule, but only because of fear of punishment or some other incentive; whereas what we really want is for people to act out of *respect* for a rule. This is what true virtue requires. (I discuss these ideas of Kant's more fully in Part III.)

We might wonder whether only a vulgarized religion should be condemned so strongly. The question then becomes, what other kind is there? A more adequate conception of God should certainly stop him from being a vindictive old man in the sky. Something more abstract, perhaps? But in that mystical direction lies a god who stands a long way away from human beings, and also from human good or bad. As the Greek Stoic Epicurus (341–271 BC) put it:

> The blessed and immortal nature knows no trouble itself nor causes trouble to any other, so that it is never constrained by anger or favour. For all such things exist only in the weak.

A really blessed and immortal nature is simply too *grand* to be bothered by the doings of tiny human beings. It would be unfitting for it to be worked up over whether human beings eat shellfish, or have sex one way or another.

The alternative suggested by Plato's dialogue is that religion gives a mythical clothing and mythical authority to a morality that is just there to begin with. Myth, in this sense, is not to be despised. It gives us symbolism and examples that engage our imaginations. It is the depository for humanity's endless attempts to struggle with death, desire, happiness, and good and evil. When an exile reminisces, she will remember the songs and poems and folktales of the homeland rather than its laws or its constitution. If the songs no longer speak to her, she is on the way to forgetting. Similarly, we may fear that when religion no longer speaks to us, we may be on our way to forgetting some important part of history and human experience. This may be a moral change, for better or worse. In this analysis, religion is not the foundation of ethics, but its showcase or its symbolic expression.

In other words, we drape our own standards with the stories of divine origin as a way of asserting their authority. We do not *just* have a standard of conduct that forbids, say, murder, but we have mythological historical examples in which God expressed his displeasure at cases of murder. Unhappily myth and religion stand at the service of bad morals as well. We read back what we put in, magnified and validated. We do not just fear science, or want to take other peoples' land, but we have examples in which God punishes the desire for knowledge, or commands us to occupy the territory. We have God's authority for dominating nature, or for regarding *them*—others different from ourselves—as inferior, or even criminal. In other words, we have the full depressing spectacle of people not only wanting to do something, but projecting upon their gods the commands making it a right or a duty to do it. Religion on this account is not the source of standards of behaviour, but a projection of them, made precisely in order to dress them up with an absolute authority. Religion serves to keep *us* apart from *them*, and no doubt it has other social and psychological functions as well. It can certainly be the means whereby unjust political authority keeps its subjects docile: the opium of the people, as Marx put it. The words of the hymn—God made the rich man in his castle and the poor man at his gate—help to keep the lower orders resigned to their fates.

If all this is right, then the death of God is far from being a threat to ethics. It is a necessary clearing of the ground, on the way to revealing ethics for what it really is. Perhaps there cannot be laws without a lawgiver. But Plato tells us that the ethical laws cannot be the arbitrary whims of personalized gods. Maybe instead we can make our own laws.

2. RELATIVISM

So instead of anything with supernatural authority, perhaps we are faced simply with rules of our own making. Then the thought arises that the rules may be made in different ways by different people at different times. In which case, it seems to follow that there is no one truth. There are only the different truths of different communities. This is the idea of relativism. Relativism gets a very bad press from most moral philosophers. The 'freshman relativist' is a nightmare figure of introductory classes in ethics, rather like the village atheist (but what's so good about village theism?). Yet there is a very attractive side to relativism, which is its association with toleration of different ways of living. Nobody is comfortable now with the blanket colonial certainty that just our way of doing things is right, and that other people need forcing into those ways. It is good that the nineteenth-century alliance between the missionary and the police has more or less vanished. A more pluralistic and relaxed appreciation of human diversity is often a welcome antidote to an embarrassing imperialism.

The classic statement occurs in Book III of Herodotus's *Histories*. The Greek historian Herodotus (from the fifth century BC) is criticizing the king Cambyses, son of Cyrus of Persia, who showed insufficient respect for Persian laws:

> *Everything goes to make me certain that Cambyses was completely mad; otherwise he would not have gone in for mocking religion and tradition. If one were to order all mankind to choose the best set of rules in the world, each group would, after due consideration, choose its own customs; each group regards its own as being by far the best. So it is unlikely that anyone except a madman would laugh at such things.*

> *There is plenty of other evidence to support the idea that this opinion of one's own customs is universal, but here is one instance. During Darius's reign, he invited some Greeks who were present to a conference, and asked them how much money it would take for them to be prepared to eat the corpses of their fathers; they replied that they would not do that for any amount of money. Next, Darius summoned some members of the Indian tribe known as Callatiae, who eat their parents, and asked them in the presence of the Greeks, with an interpreter present so that they could understand what was being said, how much money it would take for them to be willing to cremate their fathers' corpses; they cried out in horror and told him not to say such appalling things. So these practices have become enshrined as customs just as they are, and I think Pindar was right to have said in his poem that custom is king of all.*

There are two rather different elements here. One is that the law of custom is all that there is. The other is that the law of custom deserves such respect that only those who are raving mad will mock it. In our moral climate, many people find it easier to accept the first than the second. They suppose that if our standards of conduct are 'just ours', then that strips them of any real authority. We might equally well do things differently, and if we come to do so there is neither real gain nor real loss. What is just or right in the eyes of one people may not be so in the eyes of another, and neither side can claim real truth, unique truth, for its particular rules. Arguing about ethics is arguing about the place of the end of the rainbow: something which is one thing from one point of view, and another from another. A different way of putting it would be that any particular set of standards is purely conventional, where the idea of convention implies that there are other equally proper ways of doing things, but that we just happen to have settled on one of them. As the philosopher says in Tom Stoppard's play *Jumpers*, 'Certainly a tribe which believes it confers honour on its elders by eating them is going to be viewed askance by another which prefers to buy them a little bungalow somewhere.' But he also goes on to point out that in each tribe *some* notion of honour, or some notion of what it is fitting to do, is at work.

Why does Herodotus show such scorn of Cambyses? It is conventional to drive on either the right or the left, since each is an equally good solution to the problem of coordinating which side we drive. Presumably, then, just *because* of that, a latter-day Cambyses who mocked our slavish obedience to the one rule or the other would be mad. Certainly, there is only here the law of custom. But it is necessary for there to be *some* rule, and hence there is nothing at all to mock about whichever one we have hit upon.

In turn that suggests a limitation to the relativism. For now there come into view norms or standards that are transcultural. In the United States and Europe they drive on the right and in Britain and Australia on the left, but in each country there has to be one rule, or chaos reigns and traffic grinds to a halt. Funerary practices certainly vary, as Darius showed, but perhaps in every community, ever since we stopped dragging our knuckles, there have been needs and emotions that require satisfying by *some* ritual of passing. If an airliner of any nationality goes down, the relatives and friends of the victims feel grief, and their grief is worse when there is no satisfactory 'closure' or suitably dignified way of identifying and interring those who are lost. In Sophocles' tragedy *Antigone* (441 BC) the heroine is torn between two unyielding demands: she must obey the king, who has forbidden burial to his dead opponents in battle, and she must bury her brother, who was among them. The second demand wins, and not only the ancient Greeks, but we today, understand why. The play translates. Antigone's sense of honour makes sense to us.

So we are faced with a distinction between the transcultural requirement 'We need some way of coping with death' and the local implementation 'This is the way we have hit upon'. This is what qualifies the relativism. If everybody needs the rule that there should be some rule, that itself represents a universal standard. It can then be suggested that the core of ethics is universal in just this way. Every society that is recognizably human will need some institution of property (some distinction between 'mine' and 'yours'), some norm governing truth-telling, some conception of promise-giving, some standards restraining violence and killing. It will need some devices for regulating sexual expression, some sense of what is appropriate by way of treating strangers, or minorities, or children, or the aged, or the handicapped. It will need some sense of how to distribute resources, and how to treat those who have none. In other words, across the whole spectrum of life, it will need some sense of what is expected and what is out of line. For human beings, there is no living without standards of living. This certainly suggests part of an answer to relativism, but by itself it only gets us so far. For there is no argument here that the standards have to be fundamentally the same. There might still be the 'different truths' of different peoples.

We can approach the idea of universality a different way, however, and a way that brings into focus what is for many a serious moral dilemma. We saw above that toleration is often a good, and we do well to put many imperialistic certainties behind us. When in Rome do as the Romans do—but what if the Romans go in for some rather nasty doings? We do not have to lift the lid very far to find societies whose norms allow the systematic mistreatment of many groups. There are slave-owning societies and caste societies, societies that tolerate widow-burning, or enforce female genital mutilation, or systematically deny education and other rights to women. There are societies where there is no freedom of political expression, or whose treatment of criminals cannot be thought of without a shudder, or where distinctions of religion or language bring with them distinctions of legal and civil status.

Here we have a clash. On the one hand there is the relativist thought that 'If they do it that way, it's OK for them and in any event none of my business'. On the other there is the strong feeling most of us have that these things just should not happen, and we should not stand idly by while they do. We have only perverted or failed solutions to the problems of which standards to implement, if the standards end up like that.

Here it is natural to look to the language of justice and of 'rights'. There are human rights, which these practices flout and deny. But the denial of rights is everybody's concern. If young children are denied education but exploited for labour, or if, as in some North African countries, young girls are terrifyingly and painfully mutilated so that thereafter they cannot enjoy natural and pleasurable human sexuality, that is not OK, anywhere or any time. If *they* do it, then *we* have to be against *them*.

Many people will want to take such a stand, but then they get confused and defeated by the relativistic thought that, even as we say this, it is still 'just us'. The moral expressions of the last two paragraphs embody good, liberal, western standards. They are cemented in documents such as the United Nations' Universal Declaration of Human Rights (Appendix; an extract is opposite). But are they any more than just ours, just now? And if we cannot see them as more than that, then who are we to impose them on others? Multiculturalism seems to block liberalism.

We can, of course, insist on our standards, or thump the table. But while we think of ourselves as doing *no more* than thumping the table, there will be a little voice saying that we are 'merely' imposing our wills on the others. Table-thumping displays our

Article 1

All human beings are born free and equal in dignity and rights. They are endowed with reason and conscience and should act towards one another in a spirit of brotherhood.

Article 2

Everyone is entitled to all the rights and freedoms set forth in this Declaration, without distinction of any kind, such as race, colour, sex, language, religion, political or other opinion, national or social origin, property, birth or other status.

Furthermore, no distinction shall be made on the basis of the political, jurisdictional or international status of the country or territory to which a person belongs, whether it be independent, trust, non-self-governing or under any other limitation of sovereignty.

Article 3

Everyone has the right to life, liberty and security of person.

Article 4

No one shall be held in slavery or servitude; slavery and the slave trade shall be prohibited in all their forms.

Article 5

No one shall be subjected to torture or to cruel, inhuman or degrading treatment or punishment.

Article 6

Everyone has the right to recognition everywhere as a person before the law.

Article 7

All are equal before the law and are entitled without any discrimination to equal protection of the law. All are entitled to equal protection against any discrimination in violation of this Declaration and against any incitement to such discrimination.

The United Nations' Universal Declaration of Human Rights:
The First Seven Articles

confidence, but it will not silence the relativistic imp on our shoulders. This is illustrated by a nice anecdote of a friend of mine. He was present at a high-powered ethics institute which had put on a forum in which representatives of the great religions held a panel debate. First the Buddhist talked of the ways to calm, the mastery of desire, the path of enlightenment, and the panellists all said, 'Wow, terrific, if that works for you that's great.' Then the Hindu talked of the cycles of suffering and birth and rebirth, the teachings of Krishna and the way to release, and they all said, 'Wow, terrific, if that works for you that's great.' And so on, until the Catholic priest talked of the message of Jesus Christ, the promise of salvation, and the way to life eternal, and they all said, 'Wow, terrific, if that works for you that's great.' And he thumped the table and shouted, 'No! It's not a question of if it works for me! It's the true word of the living God, and if you don't believe it you're all damned to hell!'

And they all said, 'Wow, terrific, if that works for you that's great.'

The joke here lies in the mismatch between what the priest intends—a claim to unique authority and truth—and what he is heard as offering, which is a particular avowal, satisfying to him, but only to be tolerated or patronized, like any other. The moral is that once a relativist frame of mind is really in place, nothing—no claims to truth, authority, certainty, or necessity—will be audible except as one more saying like all the others. Of course that person talks of certainty and truth, says the relativist. That's just *his* certainty and truth, made absolute for him, which means no more than 'made into a fetish'.

Can we find arguments to unsettle the relativist's frame of mind? Can we do more than thump the table? If we cannot, does that mean we have to stop thumping it? We return to these questions in the final section of this book. Meanwhile, here are two thoughts to leave with. The first counteracts the idea that we are just 'imposing' parochial, western standards when, in the name of universal human rights, we oppose oppressions of people on grounds of gender, caste, race, or religion. Partly, we can say that it is usually not a question of imposing anything. It is a question of cooperating with the oppressed and supporting their emancipation. More importantly, it is usually not at all certain that the values we are upholding are so very alien to the others (this is one of the places where we are let down by thinking simplistically of hermetically sealed cultures: *them* and *us*). After all, it is typically only the oppressors who are spokespersons for *their* culture or *their* ways of doing it. It is not the slaves who value slavery, or the women who value the fact that they may not take employment, or the young girls who value disfigurement. It is the brahmins, mullahs, priests, and elders who hold themselves to be spokesmen for *their* culture. What the rest think about it all too often goes unrecorded. Just as victors write the history, so it is those on top who write their justification for the top being where it is. Those on the bottom don't get to say anything.

The second thought is this. Relativism taken to its limit becomes subjectivism: not the view that each culture or society has its own truth, but that each individual has his or her own truth. And who is to say which is right? So, when at the beginning of the last section I offered some moral remarks about the Old and New Testaments, I can imagine someone shrugging, 'Well, that's just your opinion.' It is curious how popular this response is in moral discussions. For notice that it is a conversation-stopper rather than a move in the intended conversation. It is not a reason for or against the proffered opinion, nor is it an invitation for the speaker's reasons, nor any kind of persuasion that it is better to think something else. Anyone sincere is of course voicing their own opinion—that's a tautology (what else could they be doing?). But the opinion is put forward as something to be agreed with, or at any rate to be taken seriously or weighed for what it is by the audience. The speaker is saying, 'This is my opinion, and here are the reasons for it, and if you have reasons against it we had better look at them.' If the opinion is to be rejected, the next move should be, 'No, you shouldn't think that because . . .' That is, an ethical conversation is not like 'I like ice-cream', 'I don't', where the difference doesn't matter. It is like 'Do this', 'Don't do this', where the difference is disagreement, and does matter.

Sometimes, indeed, ethical conversations need stopping. We are getting nowhere, we agree to differ. But not always. Sometimes we shouldn't stop, and sometimes we cannot risk stopping. If my wife thinks guests ought to be allowed to smoke, and I think they ought not, we had better talk it through and do what we can to persuade the other or find a compromise. The alternatives may be force or divorce, which are a lot worse. And in our practice, if not in our reflections, we all know this. The freshman relativists who say, 'Well, it's just an opinion,' one moment, will demonstrate the most intense attachment to a particular opinion the next, when the issue is stopping hunting, or preventing vivisection, or permitting abortion—something they care about.

The conversation-stopping response is tempting because of a philosophical view. This is that ethics is somehow 'ungrounded'. The view is that there is nothing to show that one view or another is right, or nothing in virtue of which an ethical remark can be true. Ethics has no subject matter. This kind of thought has a potent philosophical backing. We suppose that the world is exhausted by what *is* the case. A creating event only has to make the physical world, and everything else, including humanity, rolls out. But the physical world contains only *is* and not *ought*. So there is no fact making ethical commitments true. Nor could we detect any such fact. We can have no senses (ears, eyes, touch) for responding to ethical facts, and no instruments for detecting their truth. We respond only to what *is* true, never to what *ought* to be true. Thus nihilism, or the doctrine that there are no values, grips us, as well as scepticism, the doctrine that even if there were, we would have no way of knowing about them.

I come back to this later, in sections 20 and 21. But however the philosophy pans out, it is premature to think that discussion about who or what to admire, how to behave, or what we owe to each other should cease because of it. There must be a course between the soggy sands of relativism and the cold rocks of dogmatism.

3. EGOISM

We are pretty selfish animals. Perhaps it is worse than that: perhaps we are totally selfish animals. Perhaps concern for others, or concern for principle, is a sham. Perhaps ethics needs unmasking. It is just the whistle on the engine, not the steam that moves it.

How can we tell? Let us think about method for a moment. On the face of it, there are two fairly good methods for finding what people actually care about. One is to ask them, and gauge the sincerity of their response and the plausibility of what they say. The other is to see what they do and try to do. Neither method is infallible. People may deceive us. And they may be deceived about themselves. Incidentally, this is not, as is commonly supposed, an insight due to Freud. It has a philosophical, literary, and theological pedigree probably stretching back to the origins of thought itself. A nice early example is the idea of the Greek Stoics that all ambition is due to fear of death: if a man wants statues raised to himself, it is because unconsciously he is afraid of dying, but of course he is not likely to realize that. A permanent strand in Christian thought is that we have no insight, or even lie to ourselves, about our heart's desires.

Ordinarily, we can cope with fallibility by shrinking the likelihood of a mistake. We can check on what people say by seeing what they do. A man may present himself as a dutiful and nurturing father, and believe himself to be such. But if he never makes or takes an opportunity to be with his children, we have our doubts. Suppose, though, he does make such opportunities, and gladly takes them, and shows few or no regrets for what other pleasures he may be missing by taking them. Then the thing is settled: he cares about his children. In other cases, the diagnosis of smoke screen and hypocrisy beckons. The British government, not unlike others, currently uses the rhetoric of moral duty, civilized missions, and the rest in order to sound good about putting peace-keepers into many of the one hundred or so countries to whom it regularly and copiously sells arms. It is not too difficult to see the mask of concern for what it is. Everyone likes to have the words of ethics on their side (as Smilby illustrates on the next page).

Does our nurturing father really care for his children? Fallibility still threatens. Life and literature throw up cases where everything looks in line with one interpretation, yet another one seems to be hovering. Maybe this model father is scared of his wife, and knows that behaviour that apparently indicates concern for his children is what she expects. Or he may be scared of public opinion, or be angling for a certain kind of reputation to further his political career. We can look at the settled pattern of his behaviour as well as his sayings, and still wonder whether things are as they seem.

We can, but again we have methods to follow. Suppose the man's wife disappears, but he goes on nurturing as before. Or suppose his political career dies, yet he still carries on as a good father should. This rules out the idea that it was fear of his wife or hope of office that motivated him. The natural interpretation, that he cares for the children and enjoys being with them, is the only one to survive.

In the nineteenth and twentieth centuries, these homely methods began to lose ground. As the Stoics did, people bowed before the idea of hidden and unconscious meanings, uncovered only by a Grand Unifying Theory of human nature. The idea had one foot in 'hermeneutics' or the practice of interpretation. This was originally the enterprise of discovering hidden 'signatures' written by God into natural features, so that, for example, the shape of plants might indicate what they would cure. It also meant

3. 'This is the wall, Foster. We'd like you to knock up some sort of apt and symbolic mural—you know the sort of thing—The Chairman and Board presiding over the Twin Spirits of Art and Industry as they rise from the Waters of Diligence to reap the rich harvest of Prosperity while the Three Muses, Faith, Hope, and Charity flanked by Enterprise and Initiative, bless the Corporation and encourage the shareholders.' (Cartoon by Smilby.)

uncovering the hidden meanings behind the analogies, parables, and apparently unbelievable historical reports of Scripture. In its modern application, to the hermeneutic eye things may be similarly far from what they seem. So we get the view that pacifism conceals aggression, or a desire to help masks a desire for power, or politeness is an expression of contempt, or contented celibacy expresses a raging desire to procreate. Perhaps everything comes down to sex, or status, or power, or death—hermeneutics is very good at one-word solutions. It is also good at one-word dismissals of any rejection of its one-word solutions: the truth is repressed; it is hidden by false consciousness. In fact, the subject's resistance to any proffered hermeneutic interpretation can become an index of how true it is. The ideology becomes closed.

Keeping our feet on the ground, we should ask what distinguishes appropriate or accurate use of this method from mere fancy. The philosopher Karl Popper (1902–94) told a story about describing a case to the psychoanalyst Alfred Adler. Adler listened to the description, and unhesitatingly pronounced castration anxiety, father jealousy, desire to sleep with the mother, or whatever it was. When he had finished, Popper asked him how he knew. 'Because of my thousand-fold experience,' came the reply. 'And with this new case', said Popper, according to his own report, 'I suppose your experience has become a thousand-and-one-fold.' Grand Unifying Theories do not often stoop to offer themselves to empirical test.

We have strayed here from ethics into fascinating general issues in the theory of knowledge. I will only make one further remark. A Grand Unifying Theory can go along with good insights. It can unify otherwise disparate and puzzling human phenomena. In his famous book *The Theory of the Leisure Class* (1899), the sociologist Thorstein Veblen noticed a whole slew of strange facts along the following lines. First, itinerant workers who earn reasonable money tend to be 'showy', carrying flashy jewellery and large bankrolls, going in for high-stake poker games, and the like. Rooted peasants who could easily afford it never do so. Second, people deplore the taste of others who are just a little beneath them in wealth and social status, more than they deplore the taste of those a long way beneath them. Third, an aristocrat will prefer an able-bodied man as a butler or footman, rather than a female or someone handicapped who could do the job equally well. Fourth, a well-kept lawn or park is a good thing round a nice house.

Veblen unified these odd facts and many others with the theory that people have a need for wasteful display in order to manifest their status. The itinerant has to display this status on his person, and hence the flashy appearance. We need to shout that we are not like those just beneath us on the social ladder, for whom we might be mistaken, more than we need to shout that we are not like those a long way beneath us, for whom we won't be mistaken. The aristocrat (who might, after all, be impoverished) can better signal plenty by keeping able-bodied servants in unproductive jobs than if he keeps otherwise unemployable ones in their positions. Hence footmen and butlers. Similarly with gardens, lawns, and parks, which are beautiful just because they are ornamental and unproductive (Veblen thought the need controls aesthetic judgements as well). Veblen's insight is summed up as the doctrine of 'conspicuous consumption'. But the label is in fact a misnomer. The rooted peasant does not consume conspicuously. He does not have to, just because everyone he cares about knows to within an atom what he is worth.

The view that consumption has a lot more to do with vanity or status than we might have supposed is immediately plausible and was anticipated by many other thinkers, including Adam Smith (1723–90). But once Veblen has stated it in a more precise form, we can test it against our own experience and find if it works. It has the hallmarks of a good scientific theory. It is simple. It gives a unified explanation of otherwise diverse and disconnected patterns of behaviour. It is predictive (for instance, it would predict the pressure on the rooted peasant to put on a suit for his journey to town, where his worth is unknown). And it is falsifiable: for we might come across instances where the theory seems not to work, and it would need adjusting or abandoning in the light of them.

Most Grand Unifying Theory, and particularly what we might dub Grand Unifying Pessimism, is not so well-favoured. Consider the dispiriting view that everybody always acts out of their own self-interest. It can be very unclear what this means, but taken at face value it is obviously false. People *neglect* their own interest or *sacrifice* their own interest to other passions and concerns. This neglect or sacrifice need not even be high-minded: the moralist Joseph Butler (1692–1752) gives the example of a man who runs upon certain ruin in order to avenge himself for an insult. Friends with his interest at heart might try to dissuade him, but fail. What this man may need to do is to act *more* out of self-interest, so that anticipating his ruin checks his desire for revenge. But if his desire had been for the welfare of others, or for the preservation of the rain forest, or for the reduction of third-world debt, the fact that he was neglecting or sacrificing his own interest might have seemed irrelevant. It is what the situation calls for in his eyes, and if we share his standards, perhaps in ours as well. If he spends his fortune or ruins his health on these objects, he may regard himself as only having done what he had to do.

There is a trick to be guarded against at this point. Someone might read the last paragraph and complain: 'That is all very well if we think of someone's self-interest only in terms of money, or career, or even health. Certainly, people sacrifice these to other concerns. But then we just have agents whose *real* interest or full self-interest includes these other things: the revenge or the rain forest or the third-world debt. They are still just as self-interested as anyone else.' The reason this is a trick is that it empties the view of all content. It kidnaps the word 'self-interest' for *whatever* the agent is concerned about. But just for that reason it loses any predictive or explanatory force. With this understanding of interest or self-interest you could never say, 'Watch, the agent won't do this but will do that because, like all agents, she acts out of self-interest.' All you can do is wait to see what the agent in fact does, and then read back and boringly announce that this is where her interest lay. The move is not only boring but a nuisance, since, as Butler puts it, this is not the language of mankind. It would have us saying that if I stand back in order for the women and children to get in the lifeboat, then my self-interest lay in their being in the lifeboat rather than me. And this is just not the way we describe such an action. It appears to add a cynical reinterpretation of the agent, but in fact it adds nothing.

Perhaps surprisingly, we can see the general falsity of egoism by thinking of particular cases where it is indeed true. These are cases where an appearance of some larger concern does in fact disguise self-interest. Suppose two people give to a charity. Suppose it comes out that the charity is corrupt, and proceeds do not go to the starving poor but to the directors. And suppose that on receiving this news the first person is irritated and angry, not so much at the directors of the charity, but at the person bringing the news ('Why bring this up? Just let me be'); whereas the second person is indignant at the directors themselves. Then we can reasonably suggest that the first person prized his own peace of mind or reputation for generosity more than he cared about the starving poor; whereas the second has a more genuine concern for what goes on in the world, not for whether he is comfortable or how he stands in the eyes of others.

Fortunately, however, we are not all like the first person, or not all the time. We can be indignant at the directors, just as we are indignant at many things that go on around us. We don't always shoot the messenger, and we can want to be told the truth because it is a truth that concerns us.

4. EVOLUTIONARY THEORY

There exists a vague belief that some combination of evolutionary theory, biology, and neuroscience will support a Grand Unifying Pessimism. Indeed, most of the popular books on ethics in the bookstores fall into one of two camps. There are those that provide chicken soup for the soul: soggy confections of consolation and uplift. Or, there are those that are written by one or another life scientist: a neuroscientist or biologist or animal behaviourist or evolutionary theorist, anxious to tell that 'science' has shown that we are all one thing or another. Once more we stand unmasked: human beings are 'programmed'. We are egoists, altruism doesn't exist, ethics is only a fig-leaf for selfish strategies, we are all conditioned, women are nurturing, men are rapists, we care above all for our genes. There is good news and bad news about the popularity of this genre. The good news is that we do have a relentless appetite for self-interpretation. There is a huge desire to find patterns of behaviour, enabling us to understand and perhaps control the human flux. The bad news is that we will accord authority to anyone in a white coat, even when the science is over (for as we are about to see, talking of the significance of science is not talking science).

We should only venture into this literature if we are armed against three confusions. The first is this. It is one thing to explain how we come to be as we are. It is a different thing to say that we are different from what we think we are. Yet these are fatally easy to confuse with each other. Suppose, for instance, evolutionary theory tells us that mother-love is an adaptation. This means that it has been 'selected for', because animals in which it exists reproduce and spread their genetic material more successfully than ones in which it does not. We could, if we like, imagine a 'gene for mother-love'. Then the claim would be that animals with this gene are and have been more successful than animals having only a variant (an allele) that does not code for mother-love (this is likely to be grossly oversimplified, but it's a model that will make the point). The confusion would be to infer that *therefore* there is not really any such thing as mother-love: thus we unmask it! The confusion is to infer that underneath the mask we are only concerned to spread genetic material more successfully.

Not only does this not follow, but it actually contradicts the starting point. The starting point is 'Mother-love exists, and this is why'; the conclusion is that mother-love doesn't exist.

In other words, an evolutionary story, plausible or not, about the genetic function of a trait such as mother-love must not be confused with a psychological story unmasking a mother's 'real concern'. We should not rear a generation of children taught to turn round and say, 'You didn't really care about me, you only cared about your genes.' Perhaps nobody would make this mistake so baldly in this instance. But consider the idea of 'reciprocal altruism'. Game theorists and biologists noticed that animals frequently help each other when it would seem to be to their advantage not to do so. They asked the perfectly good question of how such behaviour could have evolved, when it looks set to lose out to a more selfish strategy. The answer is (or may be) that it is adaptive insofar as it triggers reciprocal helping behaviour from the animal helped, or from others witnessing the original event. In other words, we have a version of 'You scratch my back and I'll scratch yours'.

The explanation may be perfectly correct. It may provide the reason why we ourselves have inherited altruistic tendencies. The confusion strikes again, however, when it is inferred that altruism doesn't *really* exist, or that we don't *really* care disinterestedly for one another—we only care to maximize our chance of getting a return on our investments of helping behaviour. The mistake is just the same—inferring that the psychology is not what it seems because of its functional explanation—but it seems more seductive here, probably because we fear that the conclusion is true more often in this case than in the case of mother-love. There are indeed cases of seeming altruism disguising hope for future benefits. But there are of course cases in which it is not like this, and shown to be such by the methods of the last section. The driver gives the penniless hitch-hiker a lift; the diner tips the waiter he knows he will never see again; they each do it when there are no bystanders to watch the action.

To guard against this confusion, contemplate sexual desire. It has an adaptive function, presumably, which is the propagation of the species. But it is completely off the wall to suppose that those in the grip of sexual desire 'really' want to propagate the species. Most of the time most of us emphatically do not—otherwise there would be no birth control, elderly sex, homosexuality, solitary sex, and other variations—and many people never do. Some moralists might wish it were otherwise, but it isn't.

So, this first confusion is to infer that our apparent concerns are not our real concerns, simply from the fact of an evolutionary explanation of them.

The second confusion is to infer the impossibility that such-and-such a concern should exist, from the fact that we have no evolutionary explanation for it. This is unwarranted, for it may well be that there is no evolutionary explanation for all kinds of quirks: no explanation for why we enjoy birdsong, or like the taste of cinnamon, or have ticklish feet. The cartoon says it all.

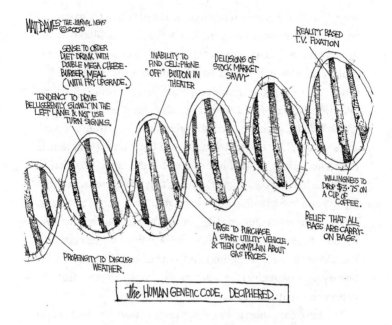

4. Matt Davies, 'The Human Genetic Code, Deciphered'.

These traits may be side-effects of others that are adaptive, or they may be descendants of traits that were once adaptive but are so no longer, or they may be nothing to do with adaptations, but just due to chance. Or they may be adaptations but only because they affect the 'eye of the beholder': perhaps it is more pleasurable to be with a partner who has ticklish feet, and then a mechanism of 'sexual selection' kicks in to boost the prevalence of the trait. That throws us back onto the question of why the pleasure and the preference exists, but perhaps it just does. Female peacocks go for the huge, beautiful, but apparently dysfunctional tails of the male, and female Irish elks went for the male practically immobilized by the biggest antlers. It is not easy to see why, and this problem can unfit explanations in terms of sexual selection for some purposes. For instance, if we find the human propensity for art or music puzzling because we cannot find a survival function for it, it doesn't immediately help to suggest that females prefer artistic and musical men, since we won't be able to find a survival function for that female preference, either. What this means is that the explanation has to continue. It might continue by showing that females recognize that artistry and musicianship indicate *other* survival-enhancing traits, such as industry or cunning (the peacock's gaudy tail may indicate freedom from disease, or the elk's antlers indicate its strength). Or, it might postulate a 'trembling hand'—a random jerk in the evolutionary process, such as the inaccurate copying of a gene, that just happened to entrench itself.

The third confusion to guard against is to read psychology into nature, and in particular into the gene, and then read it back into the person whose gene it is. The most notorious example of this mistake is in *The Selfish Gene*, by Richard Dawkins. Here the fact that genes replicate and have a different chance of replicating in different environments is presented metaphorically in terms of their being 'selfish' and indulging a kind of ruthless competition to beat out other genes. It is then inferred that the human animal must itself be selfish, since somehow this is the only appropriate psychology for the vehicle in which these little monsters are carried. Or at least, if we are not selfish, it is because by some strange miracle we can transcend and fight off the genetic pressure to be so. Dawkins has since repudiated this idea, but it maintains a life of its own.

To state this train of thought is to expose its silliness. Genes are not selfish—they just have different chances of replicating themselves in different environments. Not only may they do better if the person carrying them is unselfish, altruistic, and principled, but it is easy to see why this should be so. A society of unselfish, altruistic, and principled persons is obviously set to do better than a group in which there are none of these traits, but only a 'war of all against all'. Furthermore, the environment in which we human beings flourish is largely a social environment. We succeed in the eyes of each other. Hence, a principle like that of sexual selection kicks in: if these are traits we admire in each other, they are likely to be successful not only for the society as a whole, but also for any individual who has them. And we do admire them. We see more of the association between being good and living well in section 17.

5. DETERMINISM AND FUTILITY

The other implication of the life sciences that threatens ethics, in many peoples' minds, is the threat of determinism. The idea here is that since it is 'all in the genes', the enterprise of ethics becomes hopeless. The basket of motivations that in fact move people may not be as simple as the Grand Unifying Theories have it, but they may be fixed. And then we just do as we are programmed to do. It is no use railing about it or regretting it: we cannot kick against nature.

This raises the whole thorny topic of free will. Here, I want to look at only one particular version of the problem. This takes our genetic make-up to imply the futility of ethics, meaning in particular the futility of moral advice or education or experience. The threat is the paralysing effect of realizing that we are what we are: large mammals, made in accordance with genetic instructions about which we can do nothing.

A moral enterprise might be hopeless because it tries to alter fixed nature. A prohibition on long hair may be enforceable, say in the army or the police force. But a prohibition on growing hair at all is not, since we are indeed programmed to do it. An order forbidding hunger or thirst is futile, since we cannot control them. Some cases are less clear. Imagine a particularly ascetic monastic order, whose rule not only enjoins chastity, but forbids sexual desire. The rule is probably futile. It cannot be obeyed because it is not up to us whether we feel sexual desire. At the right time the hormones boil, and sexual desire bubbles up (lust was an object of particular horror to early Christian moralists just because of its 'rebellious' or involuntary nature). The chemical instructions are genetically encoded. There may indeed be marginal technologies of control: yoga, or biofeedback, or drugs. But for most young people most of the time, any injunction not to feel desire is futile. This is not to say that the injunction has no effect at all. It may well bring shame and embarrassment to those who find that they cannot conform to it. This may even be its function, since it may thereby reinforce their subservience in the face of the implacable authority that commanded it. It can increase the power of churches or parents to keep their dependents in a state of guilt or a state of shame. But the rule is directly futile: it cannot be obeyed. So the question is, are all rules similarly futile, because of genetic determinism?

The answer is No, because whatever our genetic make-up programs us to do, it leaves room for what we can call 'input-responsiveness'. It leaves room for us to vary our behaviour in response to what we hear or feel or touch or see (otherwise there would be little point in having these senses in the first place). It leaves room for us to vary our desires in accordance with what we learn (discovering that the glass contains sulphuric acid, I lose the desire to drink it that I had when I thought it contained gin). It leaves room for us to be influenced by information gathered from others. Finally, it leaves room for us to be affected by the attitudes of others. In other words, it makes us responsive to the moral climate.

If we liked paradox, we might put this by saying that genetics programs us to be flexible. But there is no paradox, really. Even an inanimate structure that is literally programmed can be made to be flexible. A chess program will be designed to give a different response depending on what move its opponent has just made. It is input-responsive. Inflexible traits (growing hair) are not input-responsive because no matter what beliefs, desires, or attitudes we have, they go on just the same. But many of our own beliefs and desires and attitudes are not like that. They show endless plasticity. They vary with our surroundings, including the moral climate in which we find ourselves.

It is an empirical matter how flexible we are in any particular respect. Thus, consider language. Many theorists believe that the extraordinary facility with which children pick up language requires a dedicated 'module' or structure within the brain that has this as its function. Its function is not to pick up English, German, or Latin, for any child can pick up any language. Its function is to pick up whichever language the child grows up with: its mother tongue, or tongues if it is lucky. After a time, the evidence suggests, this flexibility is substantially lost. Beyond about the age of twelve, it is almost impossible to pick up a language so as to speak it like a native. The responsiveness diminishes or vanishes. We are no longer so good at copying the inputs and finding ourselves falling in with the grammar of what we hear.

So, for all genetics tells us, a child may be disposed to become kind and loving in a kind and loving environment, vicious and aggressive in a vicious and aggressive one, intellectual and musical in an intellectual and musical one. Or, these dispositions may in turn be liable to be displaced if other factors influence things. We just have to look and see.

Very possibly, what we may find is greater receptivity at some stages, and relative inflexibility thereafter, rather as in the case of language. If this is so, far from sidelining the importance of the moral environment, the excursus through determinism will catapult it to the head of the agenda. That is where it should be if it turns out that, once we have been weaned into an atmosphere of violence, aggression, insensitivity, sentimentality, manipulation, and furtiveness—the everyday world of television, for example—we can never or almost never climb out.

There are threats of futility other than determinism. There is the mood in which all human life is futile. I discuss this in section 10.

6. UNREASONABLE DEMANDS

I have argued for moderate optimism about human nature, at least blocking the Grand Unifying Theories—the ones we called Grand Unifying Pessimisms—we have met so far. But we have to be realistic, and we should not demand too much from ourselves and each other.

Then the threat arises that ethics does just that, and not in some overblown, over-demanding version, but at its very core. And then we get the reaction that 'It's all very well in principle, but in practice it just won't work'. As Kant remarked, this is 'said in a lofty, disdainful tone, full of the presumption of wanting to reform reason by experience'. Kant finds it especially offensive, contrasting the 'dim, moles' eyes fixed on experience' with 'the eyes belonging to a being that was made to stand erect and look at the heavens'.

However, the threat is real, and we can consider several versions of it. First, consider a morality centred on a simple and abstract set of rules. One of them may be 'Thou shalt not lie'. Now of course when we think of central examples of this rule, we are apt to approve of it. We should not abuse other peoples' trust in us, and a deliberate, manipulative, barefaced lie may well do that. But there are other cases. There are white lies, socially expected and condoned. There are lies told to people who shouldn't be asking, because it is none of their business and they have no right to the truth. There are desperate lies, told because telling the truth will be catastrophic (the classic is, lying to the mad axeman who asks you where your children are sleeping). There are lies told in the service of a greater

47

truth ('There is no danger' may be literally false, but it puts the passengers in a more appropriate frame of mind than 'The risk is quite small'). There are lies we perhaps in desperation tell ourselves, and get to believe, before we tell others ('It's not the harmful kind of cancer, dear').

Some philosophers, most notoriously Kant, have grasped the nettle and forbidden even such lies. It was central to Kant's moral scheme that the prohibition remained simple and absolute: no exceptions. Suppose we agree with him. Then a perfectly reasonable reaction from anyone muddling along in society, or from the mother facing the axeman, or from the pilot calming the passengers, would be, 'To heck with that. If *that's* what morality demands, then I'm opting out.'

Here is a second example where the stringency of ethics can lead to its rejection. Many theories of ethics highlight the *impartial* and *universal* nature of the moral point of view. It is a point of view that treats everyone equally: every person has equal weight. Unless there are further factors, it is no better, from the moral point of view, that I should have some goods and you should not, than that you should have them and I should not. If the person without the goods is starving, and the person with them has plenty, then morality demands a split: the money is needed more by the starving. The starvation of the poor demands redistribution from the rich.

It is easy to preach this, but much harder to practise it. Indeed there is usually something ludicrous about the well-fed parson preaching charity, or the even better-fed academic arguing that justice is not served unless we have voluntary or involuntary redistribution programmes which carve the entire cake equally, perhaps leaving every single person just above a poverty line. If we accept, though, that morality demands this of us, then again a natural reaction is to shrug off its demands. It's not going to happen; it's impractical; we can ignore it.

I do not think it is easy to find a stable attitude to the stringency of the prohibition on lying, or still more to the duty of charity. But I do think something has gone wrong if *extreme* demands are placed squarely in the centre of ethics. The centre of ethics must be occupied by things we can *reasonably* demand of each other. The absoluteness of the fanatic, or the hair shirt of the saint, lie on the outer shores. Not wanting to follow them there, or even not able to do so, we still have plenty of standards left to uphold. We should still want to respond to the reasonable demands of decency. We may not be able to solve all the world's problems, but we should do our best with the ones we can solve. So the right reaction is to look for moral principles that are not impractical, and not limitless in their demands. Adhering to anything more stringent might be saintly, and admirable, but it is not *demanded* of us. In the standard phrase, it is above and beyond the call of duty.

A different example of a bid to escape the stringency of behaving well is the excuse of 'dirty hands'. It's a bad business manufacturing arms, or selling cattle prods to various regimes. But, says the manufacturer (or the government), if we don't do it someone else will. Then they have the jobs and reap the rewards. The arms and prods get made just the same, so why should we sacrifice our well-being for the benefit of our competitors? The moralist, standing erect and looking at the heavens, is simply out of touch with the needs of the market. Ethics is all very well, but perhaps we cannot afford it. At least the dim mole earns his living.

There is something grubby, not only to Kant but to most of us, about the excuse that this argument offers us. We have some sense that we should keep our own hands clean, however much others will then dirty theirs. The excuse is not open to a person of strict honour or integrity, however convenient it may be in practice. In many areas, it is not over and above the call of duty to keep our own hands clean.

7. FALSE CONSCIOUSNESS

In sections 3 and 4 we met Grand Unifying Pessimisms that tried to discover hidden unconscious motivations, things that really move us, leaving ethical concerns exposed as mere whistles on the engine. We resisted their claims. But there is still room to argue that the social role of morality is tainted. Even if the motivations of its practitioners are sincere enough, this is because they have been somehow sucked into a system. And the system may not be what it seems.

Consider, for instance, a feminist criticism of a piece of male behaviour. The man holds open a door for the woman, or offers to carry her parcel, or gives up a seat for her. The feminist finds this offensive. She does not have to say that the man intends to demean the woman. His behaviour, the feminist maintains, is part of a 'system' or 'pattern' of such events whose net effect is a signal that women are weaker or in need of male protection. And this she finds offensive. Of course, the man in turn may find her offence offensive, and up start political-correctness wars and gender wars.

The feminist may go in for the kind of hermeneutics we have met, saying that the man unconsciously intends to demean the woman. But that is unnecessary. She need not work at the level of individual psychology. All she has to say is that the man behaves as he does because of a system or socially institutionalized set of behaviours that are entrenched in the society, and that the function of the system is to demean women. This is enough for her critique to gain a hold.

For another example of this kind of critique, imagine a sincere cleric wringing his hands over his parishioners' sins. He is genuinely upset. He believes they are doing wrong, and fears for their souls. His heart goes out to them. There is nothing, so far, wrong with him. But he may be a part of a system with a rather more sinister function for all that. The Church that taught him may be an organization dedicated to its own power, and as we already suggested, controlling peoples' sense of shame and guilt and sin is an instrument of power. It works best if the pawns, the individual clerics, do not realize that, either consciously or unconsciously.

So a critic might now suggest that ethics as an institution (I shall write this, 'Ethics') is a system whose real function is other than it seems. A feminist might see it as an instrument of patriarchal oppression. A Marxist can see it as an instrument of class oppression. A Nietzschean may see it as a lie with which the feeble and timid console themselves for their inability to seize life as it should be seized. A modern French philosopher, such as Michel Foucault,

[margin annotation: Calls in to question whole purpose of ethics.]

can see it as a diffuse exercise of power and control. In any event, it stands unmasked.

There may be a good deal of truth in some of these critiques. We can think of local elements of morality, at particular places and times, that certainly seem open to some such diagnosis. The passion with which the rich defend the free market can invite the raised eyebrow. A morality with or without the religious fig leaf we met earlier, that gives *us* the right to *their* land, or the right to kill *them* for not having the same rituals as *us*, invites a similar diagnosis. The self-serving nature of systems of religion, or caste systems, or market systems, can be almost entirely hidden from view to those who practise them.

There is something a little off-colour, as well, about some of the ways morality sometimes intrudes into peoples' lives. The judge, or the priest, or a panel of the great and the good may tell people what they must do, but they do not usually have to live with the consequences. If the girl is not allowed the abortion, or the family not allowed to assist the suicide, they have to pick up the pieces and soldier on themselves. Those who told them how they had to behave can just bow out. An impartial moral law can bear very unevenly on different people, and it is little wonder if people become disenchanted by an ethics largely maintained by those who do not have to live it. Anatole France spoke ironically of the majestic equality of the laws which forbid rich and poor alike to sleep under bridges, to beg in the streets, and to steal bread.

Although we may well accept examples of this kind of critique, I don't think it could possibly be generalized to embrace all of ethics. The reason is implicit in what we have already said: for human beings, there is no living without standards of living. This means that ethics is not Ethics: it is not an 'institution' or organization with sinister hidden purposes that might be better unmasked. It is not the creature of some concealed conspiracy by 'them': Society, or The System, or The Patriarchy. There are indeed institutions, such as the Church or State, that may seek to control our standards, and their nature and function may need to be queried. But that will mean at most a *different* ethic. It does not and cannot introduce the end of ethics.

Every so often there arise movements for 'free living', based on doing without the restrictions and prohibitions of bourgeois morality. Usually this means in the first place free love—a natural enough ambition for some of the young. (I remember in my first year at university joining a society called the Theoretical Amoral-ists, which sounded rather rakish. To my disappointment all the other members were men. In any case, it remained theoretical.) But experimenters in free living find they face a dilemma. Either standards are introduced: standards of truth-telling, privacy, space, use of materials, job rotas, and so on, eventually apt to include property rights and rights connected with sexual bondings, or, the commune breaks up. If the scene is set so that it cannot break up (more often in fiction than real life), disaster follows.

Central elements of our standards do indeed have a function, and it may be hidden from practitioners. An ordinary person may just be shocked at a broken promise, and that is the end of it. They do not have to reflect on the function of promise-keeping. But if they do reflect, then the point of the 'institution' of promising may come into view. Its point will be something like this. By giving promises we give each other confidence in what we are going to do, thus enabling joint enterprises to go forward. That is a point we can be proud of; without something serving that point, flexible plans for coordinated action become impossible. Here the description of the hidden function is not an 'unmasking' or a deconstruction. If anything, it gives a boost to our respect for the norms surrounding promise-keeping. It shows that it is not just something about which we, the bourgeois, have a fetish. As I like to put it, it is not a debunking explanation, but a bunking one.

Other central elements of morality don't even get this kind of explanation. They are less of a human invention than is the device of giving promises. Gratitude to those who have done us good, sympathy with those in pain or in trouble, and dislike of those who delight in causing pain and trouble, are natural to most of us, and are good things. Almost any ethic will encourage them. Here there is nothing to unmask: these are just features of how most of us are, and how all of us are at our best. They are not the result of a conspiracy, any more than the enjoyment of food or the fear of death are: they just define how we live and how we want to live and want others to live. Nietzsche indeed tried to 'deconstruct' the benevolent emotions, railing against them as weak or slavish or life-denying, but the attempt is unconvincing and unpleasant, a kind of Hemingway machismo that regards decent human sympathy as unmanly.

There may be yet other threats to ethics. We can become depressed by the role of luck in our lives. Suppose two drivers go down the same road, each showing the same small degree of carelessness. One arrives safely; the other kills a child who darts out in front. This difference of luck affects how we think of them, how they think of themselves, and even the penalties imposed by society and by the law. Luck can do more to sway the ways our lives go than virtue. Yet people are curiously unwilling to acknowledge this; we relentlessly take responsibility, as the myth of original sin shows. It seems we would prefer to be guilty than unlucky.

Again, even when we live benevolent, admired lives according to the standards of our times, we can fear that had things been tougher we would have joined the fallen. If we are good, it may be because we were never tempted enough, or frightened enough, or put in desperate enough need. We can also fear the restless evil in the human heart. We know that neither success nor suffering ennobles people. In such a mood, we can be overwhelmed just by the relentless human capacity for making life horrible for others. The right reaction is not to succumb to the mood, but to reflect that the cure lies in our own hands.

PART TWO

Some Ethical Ideas

IN THE FIRST SECTION we deflected some sceptical challenges to ethics. There is more to be said, particularly about the threats of relativism, nihilism, and scepticism, which still lurk. But for the moment I turn from that in order to sketch some of the elements about which we need to think. An ethic will crystallize our attitudes to the most important events, such as birth and death. It will determine our attitude to life and what makes it worth living. It will encapsulate notions of human nature and human happiness, telling us what it is for a human life to go well. It will describe desire, and freedom, and our rights to the opportunities and powers that we need in life. None of these notions is easy. Some of them are open invitations to confusion.

8. BIRTH

Throughout human history we have had only a few ways to control how many children get born, and who they are. We could control the gene pool, up to a point, by controlling who mated with whom. This could be done directly only by selection of a partner, or socially by arrangements of marriage and norms governing it. We could control how many got born, by abstinence, and perhaps by abortion. We could also control which of those that were born got to grow up, by infanticide, or selective standards of upbringing. This is still far more important than is generally realized. The Nobel prizewinning economist Amartya Sen has calculated that there are over 100 million 'missing women' worldwide. That is, birth-rate statistics from not only the developed world, but sub-Saharan Africa as well, tell us that slightly more females should exist than males. But, in fact, there are 100 million fewer living women than we should expect—44 million fewer in China and 37 million fewer in India alone. The difference is due to inequalities in medical care and sustenance, as well as deliberate infanticide, to-gether making up the world's biggest issue of justice for women.

When we use any of these methods of control, we interfere with what would otherwise have happened. We might be said to inter-fere with nature. If 'interfering with nature' is, as some people sug-gest 'playing God' and therefore wrong, then we have always played God. But that is not as bad as it seems. In that sense, we play God as well when we put up an umbrella, interfering with the natural ten-dency of rain to wet our heads. As humans, we are bound to attempt to cope with the natural world, making things happen that otherwise would not have happened, or preventing things from happening that otherwise would have happened. The charge of playing God has no *independent* force. That is, people only raise it when the interference in question upsets them. If we have already determined that some natural process must be allowed to run unchecked, or that interfering with it is too risky or too radical, we might use the words as a way of crystallizing our worry when people propose to interfere. When anaesthetics were discovered, some moralists complained that their use was impious. It was playing God. Genetically engineered crops generate the same heat today. The question is whether the upset and the worry are well-founded. Most of us think it wasn't in the case of anaesthetics, and the jury is still out on genetically engineered crops.

As our technologies of control increase, so do the new questions about how to use them. In particular, the question of genetic control trails hideous historical baggage: that of the 'eugenic' movement, with its associated assumptions of racial superiority and racial purity, not to mention a simplistic science of heritability. Eugenics may look set to come back with a vengeance as science continues to unravel the genetic code, raising Frankenstein-like visions of human beings designed to order out of the genome parts store. But such visions are premature, at least. We saw in Part I something of the extent to which plasticity rules. The fantasy of a Hitler clone, therefore complete with fascist ambitions and a little moustache, forgets the fact that Hitler's genetic instructions, followed in a totally different environment, would have resulted in a totally different person. Or, if not *totally* different, still, nobody knows what interesting similarities would be likely to remain. Certainly not speaking German, obsessed by racial theories, or interested in politics.

Knowledge of the genome introduces decisions and questions of control and power that are less apocalyptic, although to some people disturbing enough. If a test can show that a gene for some hereditary disease is present, should the test be done? Should it be grounds for an abortion? Should it be grounds for a compulsory abortion, for instance if the resulting child would need large resources in order to live? It is hard to answer such questions in the abstract, but what we can do is address the problem we very much have with us today, and that clearly underlies a lot of unease in this area: that of abortion itself.

In this short book it is impossible to go over all the ground that has been covered in the debate over deliberate termination of pregnancy by removal and destruction of the foetus. I can only indicate some ways in which philosophical issues, and philosophical technique, impinge on the debate. In particular I want to show how the sound-bite slogans of the debate conceal those issues, or the need for that technique.

The public debate is often conducted as if this were a black or white issue, a case of absolute right or wrong. You must be either pro-life or pro-choice. You either believe in the right to life of the not-yet-born or you believe in a woman's right to control her own body. A good first philosophical question to ask might be whether this black and white may be an illusion. It may be the result of a moral lens that imposes its black and white on a landscape of different shades of grey. After all, the biological fact is that foetal development is gradual. The one-cell starting point or zygote is a different kettle of fish from the baby about to be born. But the complexity arrives gradually, hour by hour, day by day.

And then the reasons for which a woman might seek an abortion are *more or less* stringent and compelling. The poor, incompetent, frightened, raped fourteen-year-old is a different case from the socialite who would prefer to delay childbirth until after the skiing season, and a different case again is the woman wanting to abort a foetus because pre-natal testing has shown it is female.

If it were just a question of finding an appropriate attitude to abortion, we might go along with this gradualism. The woman seeking a late abortion because of the skiing would strike most of us as heartless in a rather disturbing way, just as a woman unperturbed by a late miscarriage would similarly strike us. She may, of course, turn round and say that it is none of our business, and after all there may be hidden fears or needs at work. We might not want to be too judgemental in any such cases, but we can still recognize that some reasons are more compelling than others. Perhaps for many people, especially in the liberal countries of Europe, a fairly tolerant gradualism is therefore the solution. But many cultures, including that of the United States, ratchet up the issue in two ways.

First, it is moralized, becoming not just a question of sympathy or concern, which admit of graduations, but of who has *rights*, or what *justice* requires, or what our *duty* is; it is a question of what is *permissible* and what is *wrong*. These are called 'deontological' notions, after the Greek *deontos*, meaning duty. They have a coercive edge. They take us beyond what we admire, or regret, or prefer, or even what we want other people to prefer. They take us to thoughts about what is *due*. They take us to demands.

Second, the question is often politicized, becoming a question of law. This is a step, because not all wrongdoings are criminal, and it is a political, and eventually an ethical, issue how far the law is allowed to intrude upon them. Indeed, one of the moral signatures of a society will be the extent to which the law allows liberty to do, feel, or think the wrong things. So even if we feel that there is at least a category of abortions that ought not to be performed, the question of criminalization remains open. They wouldn't be performed in an ideal world, but it is not the function of law to forbid and punish every departure from an ideal world. Even people who disapprove of alcohol may be aware that it was a very bad idea indeed to criminalize it, as was done in America in the 1920s.

It will seem natural to only one side of the debate to ratchet up the issue. It will seem natural only if we think that the issue is akin to an issue of murder. The foetus, on this view, is a person, and has a person's full rights and protections. Hence, it is a deontological issue and it is an issue for the law. But is this true?

A foetus is a potential person, certainly. But 'potential' is a dangerous word. A yellow flower is a sort of flower. But an acorn is a potential oak-tree without itself being an oak tree. My car is potential scrap, but it is not scrap, and its being potential scrap does not justify anybody in treating it as scrap.

Is the foetus not only a potential person but an actual person? What kind of question is that? A possibility is that in describing the foetus as a person, the word 'person' is itself functioning to imply a moral category, so by insisting that the foetus is a person the opponent of legal abortion is just repeating himself. Moral conclusions are frequently *presupposed* in just this way by the very terms in which the question is raised. A person, on this account, is just anything that ought to be treated as a person and afforded protection as a person. But then, whether a foetus is a person is exactly the question that is in doubt. The way in which moral conclusions are often presupposed by a choice of words was noticed long ago by the Greek historian Thucydides (c. 455–c. 400 BC). At a time of civil war, he wrote:

> To fit in with the change of events, words, too, had to change their usual meanings. What used to be described as a thoughtless act of aggression was now regarded as the courage one would expect to find in a party member; to think of the future and wait was merely another way of saying one was a coward; any idea of moderation was just an attempt to disguise one's unmanly character; ability to understand a question from all sides meant that one was totally unfitted for action.

Returning to abortion, we should note that, equally, the T-shirt slogan of a woman's right to control her own body begs the question the other way: the ways in which we may control our bodies may well depend on what other persons are dependent upon them. So if the foetus is a person, that right will be circumscribed. If a murderer is prowling around, my general right to talk is defeated by the fact that your life depends on my silence.

Rights are themselves tricky things, as we shall see further in section 15. In one of the most famous papers in this debate, Judith Jarvis Thomson compares the situation of a pregnant mother to that of someone suddenly waking to find another person plugged into them and dependent on them for life-support. She argues that the dependent person's 'right to life' does not include a right to un-limited demands on other people, including here the demand that the supporter continues her support. The value of the analogy has been challenged, but it introduces the important distinction be-tween having a right to life, and having a right to the time or labour or energies of others that, as it happens, are necessary to support that life.

Suppose, then, we look for marks of increasing approximation to a person. We will find them at different stages. We might look out for the development of a functioning brain, or a capacity for 'distress' or for movement that at least resembles the behaviour which in persons expresses pain. The foetus is not, however, a sub-ject with plans, intentions, fears, memories, or self-consciousness, each of which form part of our own adult personhood. These come later. And then it seems that there is no principled place to draw a line. The foetus, and the baby, just go on becoming *more and more* of a person. Nature is gradual, through and through.

A bad argument to watch out for now has the form: 'If there is no principled place to draw a line, then we must draw it *here*—at the very moment of conception'; or, if you stand on the woman's right to control her body, we should draw it only *there*—at the moment of birth. The idea is that anywhere else involves a 'slippery slope'. If you say that abortion is the killing of a person after five months, why not four months and three weeks? Four months and two weeks? Six months?

'Slippery slope' reasoning needs to be resisted, not just here but everywhere. It is exemplified in the paradox of the bald man, known as the Sorites paradox. A man with no hairs on his head is bald. A man who is bald is never made not bald by the addition of just one hair. Hence (working upwards one hair at a time) a man with, say, a hundred thousand hairs on his head is bald. But that is just false! Such a man is the reverse of bald. The paradox exercises logicians, but in moral and legal contexts it has no force. Consider the imposition of a speed limit. We choose a definite limit, say 30 miles per hour, and make it the law. We do not really believe that 29 miles per hour is always safe, and 31 is always not. But we would not listen to someone saying, 'There is no principled place to draw a line, so we can't have a limit.' Nor would we listen to Sorites reasoning forcing the limit forever upwards, or forever downwards to zero. So, if we think the abortion issue does need moralizing and politicizing, nothing stops us from fixing a particular term of pregnancy beyond which abortion is generally prohibited. It won't have a firm metaphysical foundation, but perhaps, like the speed limit, it doesn't need one.

To return to the question of whether the foetus is a person, consider the event of a natural miscarriage. Nature is not particularly sparing with these; they are quite common early in pregnancy, and may be very common in the first few days, when they are not necessarily noticed. They can be very distressing, depending on the hopes that had been invested in the pregnancy. But they are not distressing in the same way as the death of a person. A parent who loses a child faces one of the worst experiences anyone can go through. There is someone to mourn, someone who had a life with hopes and dreams. But a prospective mother who suffers an early miscarriage does not have someone to mourn. She can mourn the loss of *what might have been,* and she can suffer for her own lost hopes and plans. But she has known no *actual* person who is lost (this may change late in pregnancy, when the child 'makes itself known'). For this reason, although she may deserve sympathy, she is not in the same category as the mother who loses a child. Hence too, even cultures that forbid abortion do not insist on a full burial service for a dead foetus. The failure to get all the way to a birth in the family is not a death in the family.

Gradualism does not fit well with the deontological notions, which have an all-or-nothing flavour about them. Gradualism fits better with notions like things going more or less well, or people behaving more or less admirably, or more or less selfishly or callously. We might think it is better to work in terms of these notions. But when issues of life and death come into view, it is hard (for many people—but is their stance defensible?) to stay gradualist.

In any case, what's so bad about death?

9. DEATH

The Greek philosopher Epicurus had an argument that death should not be feared.

> Death is nothing to us, for that which is dissolved is without sensation; and that which lacks sensation is nothing to us.

The Stoics had reinforcements for this rather bare argument. One is to compare our state of non-existence after we die with our state of non-existence before we were born—and there was nothing to fear about that, was there? Another is to insist on the vanishing of time: death is just the same for one who died yesterday as for those who died centuries ago. This is the only way to make sense of 'eternity': death has no duration at all, for the subject. The poet Andrew Marvell may have chivvied his reluctant mistress by reminding her that 'Yonder all before us lie / deserts of vast eternity', but these are not deserts anybody (ever) crosses. In other words, 'the state of being dead' is a misnomer. The fact that Kant is dead is not the fact that Kant is in some mysterious state and is going to be for a very, very long time. It is the fact that Kant no longer exists. Death is not the state *of* a person. It is 'nothing to us' because we no longer exist. It is not a kind of life: peaceful, reposed, reconciled, content, cold, lonely, dark, or anything else.

It is often felt that death is an enigma, perhaps the ultimate mystery (see opposite). Why? Life is mysterious, insofar as it raises scientific questions. But then we have the life sciences to help us. The self-sustaining processes of life are reasonably understood. They are easily disrupted, and have finite duration. When the time comes, they cease, and what was once alive, be it a leaf or a rose or a person, dies. There is no mystery about that, beyond unravelling the chemistry and biology of it.

Death can only be thought of as mysterious when we try to understand it by *imagining* it. And then we will be imagining 'what it will be like for *me*'. But death is like nothing for me, not because

5. William Blake, 'The Soul Exploring the Recesses of the Grave'.

it is mysteriously unlike the things I have so far known, but because there is no me left.

Of course, this is so only if we deny ourselves the consolation of an afterlife. For many people, one of the attractions of the major religions is the promise of just such a life: a changed state of being, for better or worse. Ethics is one of the motivations to this belief. Life here is unjust or intolerable. So there must be a better one somewhere else. Or, it is intolerable that the unjust man meets happiness and success, and the just man meets misery and failure. So there must be another arena where justice is restored. Or, it is intolerable that some people, through no apparent fault of their own, are born to lives of want and misery. So, they must be being punished for some fault in a previous life. Such arguments sound suspiciously like wishful thinking rather than solid reasoning. Their form is: 'Things are in some respect intolerable here, so they must be better somewhere else.' But unless we are convinced of Divine purpose, the truth may be that life is in these various respects intolerable here, and that's the end of it. And, as David Hume (1711–76) argued, even if we *are* convinced of Divine purpose, there can only be one source of evidence of what it is. This must be what we find in the world around us. So if life here is unjust and intolerable, then the only defensible inference is that Divinity intends a fair dose of things that are unjust and intolerable. Job recovered in the end, but many just, upright men do not.

Many philosophers argue, and I agree, that belief in the afterlife involves an indefensible metaphysics: a false picture of how we as persons relate to our physical bodies. It imagines the soul as

6. William Blake, 'The Just Upright Man is Laughed to Scorn', from *Illustrations to the Book of Job*. Blake's Job is depicted as bearing up, but the oblique gaze of his accusers shows their blindness to his virtues.

accidentally and only temporarily lodged in a body, like a person in a car. Whereas many philosophers think of the distinction between mind and body as much more subtle than this. They might say it is more like the distinction between the computer program and the machine on which it runs. There is a distinction, sure enough, but not one that gives you any license to imagine the software running, but without any hardware at all.

If belief in life after death is abandoned, the Stoics seem clearly right that death is not to be feared. Still, we need to disambiguate a little. Kant's death was an event, and it happened to Kant. It was the end of Kant's dying. In this sense, alas, when death comes we do exist, for we have to do the dying. It is only at the end of the process that there is no subject of the process. And we may reasonably fear the process. We all hope to go quickly, and quietly, and painlessly, and with dignity. We hope not to die in terror or pain. We like the fact that people are concerned to make dying easy. We laugh nervously at reports that doctors idiotically refuse pain-killers to the dying, on the grounds that they might become addicted.

However, as Woody Allen said, 'I wouldn't mind dying so much if it wasn't that I would be dead at the end of it.' Faced with a choice between dying, and undergoing a process just the same until the very last moment, when we recover, most of us would opt for the second. It would be bad, but not as bad as the other. So perhaps we don't really follow the Stoics in our hearts. It is not only the process of dying, but the subsequent annihilation that concerns us.

Some people fear annihilation more intensely the more they enjoy life. Others become timorous and afraid as age dulls even their enjoyments. Either way, as we look forward, we might hope for and prefer more time of good company, hot dinners, concerts, and sex, to only a brief final fling. If we suffer only the pseudo-dying, once we have recovered perhaps we shall get all that extra time. So of course that is preferable to the shorter span. We can mourn what we will never do. Equally, the death of a child is a more moving event than that of an adult, because of all that the child never enjoyed and never did.

There is something mock-heroic about the stance that death is not an evil. If it is not an evil, then there seems to be a corollary, which is that there is nothing especially bad about killing; or, if there is something bad about killing, it is because it is bad for the relatives or friends. Yet the prohibition against killing has a central place in almost any morality. Even in societies which allow some killings—euthanasia, infanticide, execution of criminals or prisoners of war or political opponents—the boundaries are strict; places where they have broken down more or less entirely (currently, perhaps Sierra Leone) are places where society has dissolved.

It may be fairly easy to see why causing death should be the crime that it is. If a person is prepared to transgress against that rule, it seems that anything goes. But what then about desired death, such as suicide, or euthanasia? Perhaps the most serious argument against these is that if they are a legitimate option, people will become attracted to them, or pressured to accept them, by other people who stand to profit from their extinction. Hence, it is best to educate people to believe that these are just not an option, for otherwise those who are approaching death slowly will be put under pressure to speed things up. Myself, I cannot see this argument as very powerful. Relatives and providers can indeed pressure the elderly and powerless to do all kinds of things they don't want to do. But the belief that those closest to you would be relieved if you died is a terrible misfortune anyhow, whether or not there is the option of complying. The evil seems small and controllable, compared with the painless termination of many of the worst kinds of dying. As is often pointed out, in many countries, including England and the United States, you would be prosecuted for relieving a person from terminal suffering so bad that you would be prosecuted for *not* relieving an animal from it, by euthanasia. Why does the non-human animal deserve better than the human animal?

One issue that has much troubled moral philosophers here is the distinction between killing and letting die. Some codes of medical practice implement the old injunction, 'Thou shalt not kill, but need not strive / officiously to keep alive.' Opposition to euthanasia from within the medical profession often cites the 'volte-face' a doctor faces if, trained and accustomed to sustain life, he is suddenly asked to terminate it. On this reasoning, if a child is born terribly handicapped and needing outside support to live, or if a person is certainly dying and their life is dependent on outside support, it would be wrong to administer a lethal injection, but all right to stand by and do nothing to support their life. This may salve some consciences, but it is very doubtful whether it ought to, since it often condemns the subject to a painful, lingering death, fighting for breath or dying of thirst, while those who could do something stand aside, withholding a merciful death. One wouldn't want it for oneself, or anybody one loves. Part of the controversy here concerns whether withholding a necessity itself counts not just as letting die, but as killing. If I kidnap you and put you in my dungeon, that is not murder. But if I then withhold food, don't I murder you? In this case, I am responsible for you being dependent on me. But suppose you just happen to get into a situation where you are dependent upon me? Suppose by bad luck you just happen to be in my dungeon? Withholding food seems just as bad, or worse, than shooting you.

As a sideline, there are fascinating issues here about what causes what in any event. There is an old story about a man about to cross a desert. He has two enemies. In the night the first enemy slips into his camp, and puts strychnine in his water bottle. Later the same night, the second enemy, not knowing of this, slips into his camp and puts a tiny puncture in the water bottle. The man sets off across the desert; when the time comes to drink there is nothing in the water bottle, and he dies of thirst.

Who murdered him? Defence counsel for the first man has a cast-iron argument: my client attempted to poison the man, admittedly. But he failed, for the victim took no poison. Defence counsel for the second man has a similarly powerful argument: my client attempted to deprive the man of water, admittedly. But he failed, for he only deprived the victim of strychnine, and you cannot murder someone by doing that.

However we solve this, ethical thought seems to need some distinction between what we permit to happen and what we actually cause. These cases only show how fragile the distinction can be. The distinction fits with a deontological cast of mind, insisting that it is what we *do* that raises questions of right and wrong, justice and duty. It is as if what we *allow* to happen, or what happens anyhow, without our intervention, isn't on our criminal record. This is why it seems so important to decide which of the enemies murdered the traveller. But is it law rather than ethics that needs these cut-and-dried verdicts? Returning to the euthanasia issue, should we really admire the doctor waiting for nature to take its course, as opposed to the one prepared to bring down the curtain? Shouldn't it really be just a question of making sure that life, including the part of life that draws it to a close, goes better?

10. DESIRE AND THE MEANING
OF LIFE

Some moralists counsel that 'authentic' living means not just re-membering that one day you will die, but somehow living in con-stant awareness of that fact, 'living-unto-death'. The poet John Donne even had his own portrait painted wearing his shroud, hopefully anticipating the way he would look at the Last Judge-ment. Most of us, however, don't find Donne's preoccupation par-ticularly healthy. In fact, the mood only prevails in conditions of social instability or political impotence, corresponding to the fash-ion for pessimism and suicide among the intelligentsia. And it is hard to argue with a mood. Perhaps if the poet is half in love with easeful death, or sickened by the human carnival, he needs a change of government, or a tonic, or a holiday, rather than an ar-gument.

The mood that obsesses over death can fall into peril of incon-sistency. It is inconsistent to urge, for instance, both that death is perfectly all right, even a luxury, in itself, but that one thing that makes life meaningless and delusive is that it ends in death. For why is that a problem, if death is itself enviable?

Although the Stoics argued that death was not to be feared, they were not themselves cheerleaders for a morbid preoccupation with it. Rather, as the modern application of their name implies, theirs was a message of fortitude and resignation, or of fatalism in the face of the inevitable unfolding of events. Their attitude is en-trenched in one of the popular connotations of the word 'philosophy' itself, as in one person's comment on the misfortune of another: 'You've got to be philosophical—just don't think about it.' P. G. Wodehouse probably had the last word on this aspect of the Stoics. Jeeves is consoling Bertie:

> *'I wonder if I might call your attention to an observation of the Emperor Marcus Aurelius. He said: "Does aught befall you? It is good. It is part of the destiny of the Universe ordained for you from the beginning. All that befalls you is part of the great web."'*
>
> *I breathed a bit stertorously.*
>
> *'He said that, did he?'*
>
> *'Yes, sir.'*
>
> *'Well you can tell him from me he's an ass. Are my things packed?'*

As Bertie judiciously remarks later: 'I doubt, as a matter of fact, if Marcus Aurelius's material is ever the stuff to give the troops at a moment when they have just stubbed their toe on the brick of Fate. You want to wait till the agony has abated.'

Philosophers and poets who try to reconcile us to death usually do so not by arguments as terse as the Stoics', nor by Stoical fatalism, but on the contrary by moaning about life itself. We have all heard the woeful refrain. The human world is nothing but strife, disorder, and instability. Life is wearisome, a burden. Its hopes are delusive, its enjoyments are hollow. Desire is infinite and restless; gratification brings no peace. *Carpe diem* (seize the day)—but you cannot seize the day, for it vanishes into the past as you try. Everything tumbles into the abyss, nothing is stable; palaces and empires crumble to dust, the universe grows cold, and all will be forgotten in the end.

> *Vanity of vanities, saith the preacher, vanity of vanities, all is*
> *vanity. What profit hath a man for all his labour which he*
> *taketh under the sun?*

The dead, beyond it all, are to be envied. Death is a luxury. Best of all not to have been born, but once born, better quickly dead.

The peril here is what the philosopher George Berkeley (1685–1753) called the vice of abstraction, or 'the fine and subtle net of abstract ideas which has so miserably perplexed and entangled the minds of men'. It is much easier to lament the hollow nature and the inconsistencies of desire if we stay out of focus, keeping the terms of discussion wholly abstract. Thus, it sounds miserable if the satisfaction of desire is fleeting, and desire itself is changeable and apt to give rise only to further dissatisfactions. But is it really something to mope about? Thinking concretely, suppose we desire a good dinner, and enjoy it. Should it poison the enjoyment to reflect that it is fleeting (we won't enjoy this dinner forever), or that the desire for a good dinner is changeable (soon we won't feel hungry), or only temporarily satisfied (we will want dinner again tomorrow)? It is not as if things would be better if we always wanted a dinner, or if having got a dinner once we never wanted one again, or if the one dinner went on for a whole lifetime. None of those things seem remotely desirable, so why make a fuss about it not being like that?

If the pessimistic mood does get into focus, it is apt to concentrate on problematic desires, such as the desire for wealth, or, perhaps, erotic desire. It is easy to argue that these are intrinsically un-satisfiable, at least for some people some of the time. The achieve-ment of wealth often brings either the demand for more, or the inability to enjoy what we have. Our well-being can certainly be destroyed by poverty, but the briefest look at the lives of the rich does not suggest that well-being is increased without end by fur-ther riches. Many people in the world are much richer than any people used to be, but are they happier? Relevant social measures, such as suicide rates, certainly do not suggest so. The walled and guarded ghettoes of the rich, such as American Governor's Club enclaves, scarcely testify to happy, enviable lives. And, following Veblen, we might expect that increasing national income simply raises the baseline from which vanity requires the rich to distin-guish themselves. This is one of the dismal things about the dismal science of economics (see the illustration on the next page).

The other trump card of the pessimists, erotic desire, is notori-ously restless and insecure, and apt to deliver only partial fulfil-ments. Perhaps we never quite possess another person as much as we really desire to. Art has had little difficulty connecting erotic de-sire with the yearning for death and annihilation. Love itself is a kind of death—the lover is penetrated or stricken. In this tradition, the languors of love, and especially the orgasm (in French, *une petite mort*, 'a little death'), are symbols for a real death. It is argued that the deaths in works such as *Tristan and Isolde* or *Romeo and Juliet* indicate the concealed desire of lovers for joint extinction. In art it is extraordinarily dangerous to be a female in love, as the endless procession of Ophelias, Violettas, Toscas, and Mimis reminds us.

7. Richard Hamilton, 'What Is It that Makes Today's Homes So Different, So Appealing?'

It is very depressing to suppose that even *eros* (desire) is infected by *thanatos* (death). But perhaps the vice of abstraction is at work again. Concentrating on some works of art, we conclude that 'erotic desire has death at its centre'. We do not pause to reflect that it was the artist who needed the theme of the doomed lovers,

78

suppressing reference to any ordinary, everyday pleasures and contentments. The artist has good reason to dress Jack and Jill up as Romeo and Juliet. But by themselves Jack and Jill are probably a good deal more cheerful. Doom is neither inevitable, nor, usually, desired.

We similarly abstract when we ask whether life, en bloc as a single lump, 'has a meaning', imagining, perhaps, some external witness to it, which may even be ourselves from beyond the grave, looking back. We may worry that the witness has the whole of time and space in its gaze, and our life shrinks to nothingness, just an insignificant, infinitesimal fragment of the whole. 'The silence of those infinite spaces terrifies me,' said Blaise Pascal (1623–62).

But the Cambridge philosopher Frank Ramsey (1903–30) replied:

> Where I seem to differ from some of my friends is in attaching little importance to physical size. I don't feel the least humble before the vastness of the heavens. The stars may be large, but they cannot think or love; and these are qualities which impress me far more than size does. I take no credit for weighing nearly seventeen stone.
>
> My picture of the world is drawn in perspective, and not like a model to scale. The foreground is occupied by human beings, and the stars are all as small as threepenny bits.

When we ask if life has meaning, the first question has to be, to whom? To a witness with the whole of space and time in its view, nothing on a human scale will have meaning (it is hard to imagine how it could be visible at all—there is an awful *lot* of space and time out there). But why should our insignificance within that perspective weigh on us? Suppose instead we have in mind a more down-to-earth audience. Someone spending his life on some goal, such as the cure for cancer, may worry whether his life has meaning, and the worry will be whether it has meaning to those for whom he is working. This will be so if his work is successful, or if the generation coming up will remember it. For some people, the thought that their work may eventually fail, and give them no memorial, is extremely painful. Others manage to be quite cheerful about it: after all, very, very, few of the world's people leave behind achievements that excite the continuing admiration of the next generation, let alone generations beyond. This is sadly true even in philosophy departments.

Perhaps we put ourselves in the position of the judge: each of us can ask whether life has meaning to *me*, here and now. The answer then depends. Life is a stream of lived events within which there is often plenty of meaning—for ourselves, and those around us. The architect Mies van der Rohe said that God is in the details, and the same is true of meaning in life to us, here, now. The smile of her child means the earth to her mother, the touch means bliss for the lover, the turn of the phrase means happiness for the writer. Meaning comes with absorption and enjoyment, the flow of details that matter to us. The problem with life is then that it has too much meaning. In other moods, however, everything goes leaden. Like Hamlet, we are determined to skulk at the edge of the carnival, seeing nothing but the skull beneath the skin. It is sad when we become like that, and once more we need a tonic more than an argument. The only good argument is, in a famous phrase of David

Hume's, that it is no way to make yourself useful or agreeable to yourself or others.

11. PLEASURE

With the starting, ending, and meaning of life in place, we still may want to consider how it is to be lived. There are different ways of going about this. The first we shall consider goes by sketching some conception of the good life, the *summum bonum* (maximum good). We imagine an ideal life, and fill in its details accordingly: perhaps it is happy, it is joyous, it contains achievements of love and friendship and activity, it has no desires it cannot fulfil, it is sufficient to itself. It is the *enviable* or, if the word is a little negative, the *admirable* life. It is the life of what Aristotle (384–322 BC) called *eudaimonia*.

This is usually translated as 'happiness', but there are pitfalls in that. Happiness, in the modern mind, is often sketched as a state of purely 'subjective' or internal pleasure. A happy life is a string of satisfying inner sensation. The philosopher Jeremy Bentham (1748–1832), the principal founder of utilitarianism, saw it like that. He believed that a pleasure could be measured by putting together various factors: its subjective intensity, its duration, the probability of its happening, its nearness or remoteness from an agent in time, and its effect on producing or inhibiting yet further pleasures. Summing up the calculation over all affected parties, one could then simply calculate which course of action would (probably) produce the most pleasure and least pain. This ⋯ ⋯ ⋯ be the right thing to do: in the famous phrase, it would be the act that would probably produce 'the greatest happiness of the greatest number'.

There is something a bit deflating about Bentham's picture. It suggests a life of monotonous hedonism, fit only for pigs. Yet surely 'better Socrates dissatisfied than a pig satisfied'. This criticism can be deflected, however. Bentham's follower John Stuart Mill (1806–73) argued that it is the critic who insinuates that human beings are no better than pigs. For it is the critic who claims that our only pleasures are those of animal sensation. A more optimistic picture reminds us of the pleasures of friendship, achievement, art, music, Socratic conversation, and discovery. Mill had the somewhat Victorian view that people who have sampled these higher pleasures inevitably prefer them. He ought to have said that this just meant they were more pleasurable, but he muddied the waters by introducing the different dimension of the 'quality' of pleasure. This betrays Bentham by introducing some other source of value than pleasure itself, as if having said that price is the only measure of the merit of a painting, you go on to say that some expensive paintings are of less merit than cheaper ones. Bentham himself could only allow a notion of the 'quality' of pleasure insofar as some pleasures are midwives to yet further pleasures, whereas others trail miseries in their wake. Mill's main point remains, though, that anybody concentrating upon happiness or pleasure can remember the indefinite variety of things in which human beings take pleasure, or the indefinite variety of things they enjoy.

Bentham's ambition of a 'felicific calculus'—a scientific way of measuring what matters in decisions—was inherited by economics. But it is the nature of pleasures to resist measurement: the subjective intensities of different pleasures seem incomparable, even in one person, and across persons and times the problem is worse. A more tractable alternative is to try to measure how much people want things, and then to measure how well life is going by seeing how many of their desires are satisfied. However, one need not be very high-minded to reject this measure as well. A life of continuous gratification of desire may be better, other things being equal, than one where the same desires were not gratified. But what if the desires are trashy, stoked up by false promises and allurements, motivated by vanity and self-esteem? What if their gratification turns to ashes? Do things go better when people gratify trivial desires that were induced in the first place by playing on their fears or fantasies? What about the gratifications of the gambler or the drug addict (see the illustration on the next page)?

This introduces the Aristotelian alternative to Bentham. For Aristotle, a long succession even of pleasurable inner sensations cannot make up genuine happiness, or *eudaimonia*. 'Inner sensations' could be generated or sustained by living in a fool's paradise. A person might be happy, in this sense, when her desires are unfulfilled, but she doesn't realize it, or her pleasure derives from misunderstanding or deception. Her partner deceives her, but she doesn't know it; her children fail, but she is told they succeed; she believes she has the admiration of others, but they laugh at her behind her back. She happily expects Paradise, but there is no Paradise. If someone dies like this, then Bentham would sum up her life as happy. But in Aristotle's sense, she did not die happy.

8. William Hogarth, 'The Cock Fight'.

Hers has not been an enviable or admirable life. It is not one we would wish for ourselves. When we have been ignorant or deceived, the Aristotelian verdict, looking back, would be that we thought we were happy when we were not. We had the illusion of happiness. True happiness in this sense requires some correct relationship with our world. It cannot be gained by stoking up sensations within. In the same way, a succession of pleasures, a life of endless release of endorphins, perhaps through some chemical stimulation, would not be a life of Aristotelian happiness. It is not one we could admire or envy or wish for those whose happiness we care about.

The Aristotelian alternative requires engagement with the world. It requires reasoning and activity, and engagement with others, and notably it requires real love and friendship. For Aristotle this is because we have a *telos* or 'end'. It is the 'purpose' and therefore the 'good' of human beings to lead a certain kind of social life. The essential comparison is with health. The *telos* of a living thing is to live what counts as a healthy life for things of that kind. So our *telos* will be to live what counts as the healthy life for a human being, our 'natural' life or 'intended' life.

We may find it difficult to recapture Aristotle's sense of a purpose built into nature. But we can give ourselves an approximation by means of the idea of a biological function. The healthy life will be one in which everything is functioning as evolution has adapted it to function. That is the 'intended' life for a biological organism. It is life according to the 'natural law' of human life.

It has to be said that all these concepts are very problematic. Some people have thought that the 'natural law' of human life is ferocious competitive struggle, with little room for virtues such as altruism and justice. It is very hard to recapture any robust sense of what nature intends for us, given the plasticities of environment and culture that we have already touched upon. Furthermore, we are used to the idea that a lot of modern living is 'unnatural'—but for that very reason better than anything nearer to nature. Few of us want to return to being hunter-gatherers. Books, concerts, and bicycles are unnatural, but components of many a good life. Conversely, there is nothing particularly virtuous about confining ourselves to 'natural' diets or 'natural' ways of locomotion, or shelter, or sexual behaviour.

We could expand our concept of the natural, arguing, for instance, that since nature has equipped us with a huge general-purpose intelligence, anything produced using that intelligence should count as natural and therefore healthy. Just as all languages are equally natural, so all expressions of the general-purpose intelligence are. But this is not going to select out just some pleasures or some ways of living as especially healthy for human beings. Our intelligences can lead us to the destruction of ourselves and others just as quickly as they lead to health and flourishing. The gardens of the human condition contain some pretty depressing areas (as Leunig shows us, opposite). We will need to remember these cautions when we return to Aristotle as someone who potentially provides 'foundations' for ethics in section 17.

12. THE GREATEST HAPPINESS OF THE GREATEST NUMBER

We met in the previous section the formula of the greatest happiness of the greatest number. Utilitarianism is the moral philosophy putting that at the centre of things. It concentrates upon general well-wishing or benevolence, or *solidarity* or identification with the pleasures and pains or welfare of people as a whole. This is the impartial measure of how well things are going in general. The good is identified with the greatest happiness of the greatest number, and the aim of action is to advance the good (this is known as

9. Leunig, 'Gardens of the Human Condition'.

the principle of utility). Utilitarianism is *consequentialist*, or in other words, forward-looking. It looks to the effects or consequences of actions in order to assess them. In this it contrasts with deontological ethics. For consequentialism, an action that might be thought wrong, or undutiful, or unjust, or a trespass against someone's rights, might apparently be whitewashed or justified by its consequences, if it can be shown to be conducive to the general good. Utilitarianism fits better with the 'gradualist' approach to ethical issues, illustrated above in the case of abortion. It deals with value—with things being good or bad, or better or worse—as the greatest happiness of the greatest number increases or diminishes.

Deontological notions of justice, rights, duties, fit into a moralistic climate, where things just *are* right and wrong, permissible or punishable. These are the words of law, as much as words of ethics. Utilitarianism by contrast gives us the language of social goods. A utilitarian, faced with the issue of abortion, would look at the social conditions leading people to want abortions in the first place. Asked about a law, a utilitarian would wonder what benefits and harms arise from the criminalizing of activities. The cast of mind is that of the engineer, not the judge.

John Stuart Mill thought he had some kind of proof of the principle of utility. He thought desiring a thing and finding it pleasant are one and the same. So each individual is concerned, always and solely, for things only insofar as they are pleasant to that individual. So it follows, somehow, that everyone in general is concerned for everyone's pleasure, or for the general happiness. This is another of those cases where the argument is so bad that the conclusion not only fails to follow, but actually seems to contradict the starting point. It is like arguing that since each person ties just his or her own shoelaces, everyone ties everyone's shoelaces. But alas, except in a world of one person, if each person ties just his or her own shoelaces, *nobody* ties everyone's shoelaces. Similarly, if we each desire what is pleasant to ourselves, then nobody desires what is pleasant to others, *unless* the pleasure of others is somehow an equal object of pleasure to each of us. This would be a world of indiscriminate universal sympathy: a nice world, but not quite the world we live in. People typically desire that they themselves get an enjoyment more than they desire that someone else gets it.

Even without the dubious help of Mill's argument, we can still appreciate the aim of maximizing the general happiness. This aim is forward-looking, impartial, and egalitarian: everyone counts for one, and nobody for more than one. It is an aim we want people to have. This recognition is very old: benevolence or *jen* is the supreme virtue of Confucianism. And in public affairs it has a very respectable pedigree. It is an old legal maxim that 'Salus populi suprema lex'—the safety of the people is the supreme law. If safety includes freedom from a lot of evils, and if that freedom in turn makes up welfare or happiness, then we are close to utilitarianism.

Any decent ethic would want to cry up some virtue of benevolence, or altruism, or solidarity with the aim of increasing welfare and diminishing misery for everyone. The question is whether this is the only measure, so that everything else, and in particular the deontological notions we have already met, are subordinate to this goal. Just as a lot of crimes are committed in the name of liberty, so they can be committed in the name of the common happiness. Suppose just a little bit more happiness is obtained by trampling on someone's rights. Do we have to approve of that? Is justice itself subordinate to the general good? What if it creates more happiness to give a benefit to Amy, who does not deserve it, than to Bertha, who does?

It can sound repugnant to think that we should balance justice against consequences, even when the consequences are impartial and general, and measured in terms of the most sophisticated notion of happiness we can describe. Perhaps part of us wants to thrill to a rival slogan: 'Fiat justitia et ruant coeli'—let justice be done though the heavens fall.

We seem to have a stark opposition between two slogans: 'Fiat justitia . . .' versus 'Salus populi . . .' The great David Hume responded by splitting the difference. The answer suggested by Hume's own analysis has become known as 'indirect' utilitarianism. Rules, including rules of property, promise-keeping, and rules concerning rights in general, are justified by their impact on the general happiness. The law is justified by the safety of the people. But this does not mean that the rules or the laws must *themselves* be forward-looking, always contingent upon the benefits to be obtained on the occasion. The system is artificial. It has a utilitarian justification, but the application of the rules in particular cases does not.

For a parallel, consider the rules of a game. The game may be there for a purpose—say, to provide pleasure for the spectators and the players. But the rules of the game determine how it is conducted. The rules are not to be bent on occasion, if the referee supposes that more pleasure will accrue to the spectators or players by the cheat. If people know that this is likely to happen, their whole attitude changes, and the game may become impossible. The inflexibility of the rules is one thing that makes the game possible. Similarly, says the indirect utilitarian, we can only gain the general happiness, and particularly components of it such as security, by implementing fairly inflexible rules. We give each other property rights, fixed laws that bring determinate and foreseeable justice, and we instil general dispositions to conduct that can be relied upon, whatever the circumstances.

Or perhaps we should say, almost whatever the circumstances.

Hume pointed out that when things are bad enough, rights that would otherwise stand firm give way:

> *What governor of a town makes any scruples of burning the suburbs, when they facilitate the approaches of the enemy?*

In a sufficient emergency, even quite basic civil liberties properly go to the wall. In an emergency, for instance, to get the spectators out of the threatened stadium, a referee might properly give a false call to terminate the game. But emergencies are rare, and it requires judgement to know when one is upon us. Emergencies permit exceptions, because the old stabilities and certainties can be reborn as soon as the emergency is over. A governor who burned the suburbs in wartime does not forfeit his general standing as protector of the laws, whereas one who appropriates a house during peacetime for his favorite nephew does. The one can still be trusted, whereas the other cannot.

For Hume, therefore, the edifice of justice and rights is a social creation. It is necessary, for human beings cannot manage without each other, and the structures are needed for cooperation with each other. These include at least the ability to give contracts, and the ability to hold property, and each of these needs describing in the language of deontology—justice and rights. These are there purely to promote and protect the good of society. They are necessary, but, when things get too bad, they are subordinate to that same end.

Are we happy with that subordination? Indirect utilitarianism is a kind of compromise. It is consequentialist overall, but in the conduct of life, just as in the conduct of a game, rules and principles have the paramount authority that deontologists wish. Like many compromises, it gets sniped at from each side. Utilitarians of a more direct, down-to-earth stripe may worry about the rationale for following a rule in a case where even a little utility is gained by bending it. Isn't this just making a fetish of the rule: 'rule-worship'?

Most contemporary moral philosophers are much more admiring of justice and rights, and fear their contamination by anything so vulgar as an aim or purpose. Hence it has become fashionable in moral philosophy to jeer at utilitarianism. Some writers stress virtuous agents whose integrity does not allow them to compromise principles for utilitarian ends. Others stress the virtue of agents who do not look forward to what good may come of their actions, but look backward, and apply principles to the context of action. The literature is full of lurid cases in which the man (or woman) of principle stands fast, and admirably so. But indirect utilitarianism looks set to cope with these: *of course* we value the person of integrity who cannot compromise his or her principles for the sake of general utility. For this is far the best disposition to cultivate and to admire, even if, very, very rarely, the spectators perish in the stadium because of it.

Some people stress that utilitarianism 'does not take seriously the separateness of persons'—the idea being that it subordinates the rights of the individual to solidarity with the general welfare. It is too deaf, according to these critics, to the plaintive cry coming from a particular individual whose concerns have been sacrificed to the general good. This charge is particularly ironic given that utilitarianism started with the ambition of breaking down the

FREEDOM FROM THE BAD

separateness of persons—the separateness that gives a person no concern for *us* as apart from *me.*

Other critics stress the way we might want to moralize happiness in the first place, substituting Aristotelian *eudaimonia* for anything more like Bentham's strings of sensation. And once happiness is itself moralized, the credentials of utilitarianism as an overall theory of ethics are compromised. It requires a moral vision, derived from somewhere else, to judge when things are going happily or not.

It is not difficult to hear the cries of a (largely male) mandarin class defending itself in a lot of this. An ethic of care and benevolence, which is essentially what utilitarianism is, gives less scope to a kind of moral philosophy modelled upon law, with its hidden and complex structures and formulae known only to the initiates. And utilitarianism, particularly in its indirect forms, has one enormous advantage. It at least explains how to judge whether particular rights, or rules, or even virtues of conduct, *get to be on the list* of rights, rules, or virtues. They are there because they serve the common good. Other philosophies, lacking such a sensible and down-to-earth answer, must either duck the question or struggle to find different answers. I introduce some such attempts in Part Three.

13. FREEDOM FROM THE BAD

Another approach to what matters in living well is to consider what has to be avoided. It is much easier, to begin with, to agree on this list. We don't want to suffer from domination by others, or powerlessness, lack of opportunity, lack of capability, ignorance. We don't want to suffer pain, disease, misery, failure, disdain, pity, dependency, disrespect, depression, and melancholy. Hell was always easier to draw than heaven.

The list is of most use to political philosophy. If we try to sketch what is required of a social order, it is much easier to say what has to be avoided, than what has to be achieved. A political order cannot do everything: it cannot guarantee a life free from depression or disease or disappointment. But it can give freedom from violence, discrimination, arbitrary arrest, inhuman or degrading punishment, unfair trials, and other evils. It can guarantee that you have the protection of the laws if you speak your mind (on some things) or peacefully demonstrate (sometimes). In this view, the moral or political or social order sets the scene. It can't help what people make of the scene. Whether people can go on to achieve the life of *eudaimonia* is up to them. It is not the job of a moral philosophy, and more than that of a constitution or a government, to make people happy, but only to set a stage within which they *can* be happy. The American Declaration of Independence talks of 'life, liberty and the pursuit of happiness', not the achievement of happiness.

This conception of the role of the political order is characteristic of liberalism. It is often said that its eyes are fixed on 'negative liberty'—people are to be free *from* various evils. This is contrasted with a more goal-driven or idealistic politics in which the aim is to enable people to *do* various good things or to *become* or *be* something desirable—positive liberty. But this may not be the best way of putting things, since any full specification of a freedom is apt to indicate both what you are free from and what you are free to do. A freedom *from* arbitrary arrest, for instance, is a freedom *to* do everything except some circumscribed range of things counting as crimes, without being arrested. A freedom *to* assemble peacefully is a freedom *from* legal prohibition of peaceful assembly. A freedom *from* taxation is a freedom *to* spend everything you earn without giving any to the government.

Nevertheless the contrast reminds us of something distinctive of liberalism, and of more intrusive political systems that depart from it. The more intrusive systems, such as socialism, communism, or fascism, are driven by some thicker vision of what is good than sheer freedom from legal or political interventions. So, for instance, an egalitarian might find it necessary to compromise some freedom of economic activity in order to bring about the desired outcome of rough economic equality. Many governments will compromise freedom of peaceable association if they suspect that the function of the association is to exacerbate hatreds and tensions within the society. Hegel found true freedom only in fairly rigorously structured political association, leading to the liberal Bertrand Russell's (1872–1970) gibe that, for Hegel, freedom means the right to obey the police (and see Delacroix, on the next page).

It can sound as if this is a simple clash, for instance between those who prioritize liberty and those who prioritize something else, such as peace or equality. But the language of liberty and freedom is apt to be confusing in these areas. For the word 'freedom' is flexible enough to cover the goals as well: freedom of economic activity is compromised in order to bring about freedom from economic disadvantage; freedom of association is compromised in

10. Eugène Delacroix, 'Liberty Leading the People'. But where to? (Whither?)

order to bring about freedom from tension and hatred. Almost any positive good can be *described* in terms of freedom from something. Health is freedom from disease; happiness is a life free from flaws and miseries; equality is freedom from advantage and disadvantage. The word is itself available to everyone, leading to the kind of result in the historian Gibbon's (1737–94) dry remarks about the Roman Emperor Augustus:

> *Augustus was sensible that mankind is governed by names; nor was he deceived in his expectation, that the senate and people would submit to slavery, provided they were respectfully assured that they still enjoyed their ancient freedom.*

Faced with this flexibility, the theorist will need to prioritize some freedoms and discount others. At its extreme we may get the view that only some particular kind of life makes for 'real freedom'. Real freedom might, for instance, be freedom from the bondage of desire, as in Buddhism and Stoicism. Or it might be a kind of self-realization or self-perfection only possible in a community of similarly self-realized individuals, pointing us towards a communitarian, socialist, or even communist ideal. To a laissez-faire capitalist, it is freedom from more than minimal necessary political and legal interference in the pursuit of profit. But the rhetoric of freedom will typically just disguise the merits or demerits of the political order being promoted.

Although freedom from various obvious evils is an easy goal to agree upon, it is no accident that the main traditions in moral philosophy also deal in the more positive concepts of happiness or *eudaimonia* or self-realization. For the absence of pains and miseries is, by itself, too grey and neutral to excite our ambition and admiration. Of course, it may be far more urgent, for many people much of the time, to remove the bad things than to worry a great deal about which good things we would like to succeed them. But we can't entirely do without a vision of what life would be like at its best.

14. FREEDOM AND PATERNALISM

The flexibility of the term 'freedom' undoubtedly plays a huge role in the rhetoric of political demands, particularly when the language of rights mingles with the language of freedom. 'We have a right to freedom from . . .' is not only a good way, but the best way to start a moral or political demand.

Freedom is a dangerous word, just because it is an inspirational one. The politics appropriate for societies of free individuals are above all democratic. The enemy here would be any elitism, or paternalism, supposing that some particular kinds of people, through superior reason or knowledge or wisdom, are best fitted to govern the rest, since they know peoples' interests (their *real* interests) better than the people themselves do. The elitist doctrine is that the freedom of the ignorant and those with no self-control is just frightening and useless *licence*. The most celebrated account of the elitist image is due to Plato's *Republic*. In the argument of that book, government should be in the hands of disinterested and selfless rulers or guardians who have been rigorously educated into wisdom. The mob has no right of self-determination. It is there to be governed; it is not to be allowed to find its own way of life or make its own mistakes. (Grosz seems to agree; see opposite.)

We might disapprove of Plato and approve of the democratic upshot. But we may want to be a bit nervous of the sustaining myth associated with it. The modern emphasis on freedom is problematically associated with a particular self-image. This is the 'autonomous' or self-governing and self-driven individual. This individual has the right to make his or her own decisions. Interference or restraint is lack of respect, and everyone has a right to respect. For this individual, the ultimate irrationality would be to alienate his freedom, for instance by joining a monastery that requires unquestioning obedience to a superior, or selling himself

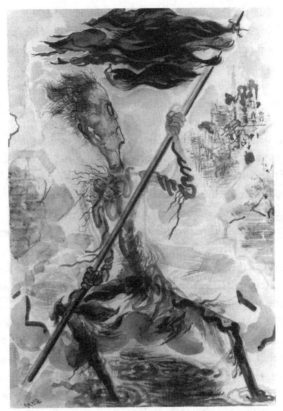

11. George Grosz, 'Waving the Flag'. Grosz comments on the ideal illustrated by Delacroix (fig. 10).

into slavery to another. Such an action would amount to a kind of suicide, a defeat of what makes each human being unique and equally valuable.

The self-image may be sustained by the thought that each

individual has the same share of human reason, and an equal right to deploy this reason in the conduct of his or her own life. Yet the 'autonomous' individual, gloriously independent in his decision-making, can easily seem to be a fantasy. Not only the Grand Unifying Pessimisms, but any moderately sober reflection on human life and human societies, suggest that we are creatures easily swayed, constantly infected by the opinions of others, lacking critical self-understanding, easily gripped by fantastical hopes and ambitions. Our capacity for self-government is spasmodic, and even while we preen ourselves on our critical and independent, free and rational decisions, we are the slaves of fashion and opinion and social and cultural forces of which we are ignorant. It would often be good, and no signal of disrespect to ourselves, if those who know better could rescue us from our worst follies.

Perhaps, then, a more realistic defence of the freedoms we want to protect avoids the fantasy of our rational freedom. A more realistic defence might be just glum about the possibility of Plato's elite. The old question from the Roman writer Juvenal's sixth *Satire* (c. AD 116) surfaces: who shall guard the guardians? Winston Churchill is supposed to have said that democracy is the worst system of government ever invented—except for all the others. Nobody can be trusted to have unlimited power over another, nor to govern in the interests of others. The elite are human too. The grim histories of anti-democratic politics stand as awful reminders of the dangers in Plato's aristocratic myth. Plato himself perfectly well knew this about the real world. The guardians of his imagined world can only merit their role by an impracticable process of the most rigorous education. Plato does not provide any consoling

myth at all for the jumped-up dictator who claims to know what is
best for the people. Democratic politicians may be bad enough,
but those sheltering behind a claim to know what is best for us are
apt to be a lot worse.

Even in democracies, however, there are fascinating relics of the
Platonic image of the guardians. The democratic United States has
its process of 'judicial review', whereby the legal mandarins of the
Supreme Court oversee and strike out democratically voted legislation. This is done in the name of the Constitution, this being a
document to whose meaning the legal mandarins alone have privileged access. The parallel with a priesthood and its private access
to the truth of the sacred texts is lost on many.

A dislike of elitism is also, typically, a dislike of paternalism: of
being told what to do in our own interest. We naturally think of
ourselves as the best judges of our own interest, and this will be
part of our conception of ourselves as self-governing, rational individuals. On the other hand, in our hearts we know that sometimes it is better if our judgements are overridden, just as it is better
for children that theirs are sometimes overridden. Safety legislation makes the worker wear a helmet or a safety harness, whether
he wants to or not. Social security systems make people pay
towards their support in old age, whether they want to or not. Most
people accept seat-belt and motorcycle-helmet laws. These all
represent restrictions on an agent's freedom made in the name of
the agent's own good. But as we have seen, we can always reinvoke
the word in explaining what the restrictions are good for. Social
security gives us freedom from poverty in old age; safety laws give

us freedom from death and destruction due to risks which we are apt to ignore.

As in the abortion debate, a little awareness of ethics will make us mistrustful of sound-bite-sized absolutes. Even sacred freedoms meet compromises, and take us into a world of balances. Free speech is sacred. Yet the law does not protect fraudulent speech, libellous speech, speech describing national secrets, speech inciting racial and other hatreds, speech inciting panic in crowded places, and so on. In return, though, we gain freedom from fraud, from misrepresentation of our characters and our doings, from enemy incursions, from civil unrest, from arbitrary risks of panic in crowds. For sure, there will always be difficult cases. There are web sites giving people simple recipes on how to make bombs in their kitchens. Do we want a conception of free speech that protects those? What about the freedom of the rest of us to live our lives without a significant risk of being blown up by a crank? Many feminist philosophers argue that pornographic speech interferes with the freedom of women to live without being the objects of demeaning fantasy. This is an important freedom, for we have several times touched on the way in which the respect we have in the eyes of others is a component of happiness. But how does it stack up against the freedom of others, men and women, to communicate their fantasies, regrettable though those may be? It would be nice if there were a utilitarian calculus enabling us to measure the costs and benefits of permission and suppression, but it is hard to find one.

15. RIGHTS AND NATURAL RIGHTS

At the beginning of the last section we noticed how 'We have a right to freedom from . . .' is not only a good way, but the best way to start a moral or political demand.

Yet it also seems to suggest a recipe for boundless expansion: we can hear people demand, without blushing, a right to freedom from any disadvantage, unhappiness, offence, want, need, disappointment . . . It sounds desirable, until we reflect that the other side of a right in these contexts is a duty: a duty on the legal or political or economic order to protect them from disadvantage and the rest. And then we need to wonder whether it is just too costly, or not even possible, for us to labour under those duties.

The United Nations' Universal Declaration of Human Rights arguably falls into this trap sometimes. In addition to the civil rights we would presumably all wish to protect, it introduces a number of 'welfare rights'. It says, for example, that everyone has a right to realization of 'the economic social and cultural rights indispensable for his dignity and the free development of his personality'. This opens the door to just the inflation described: it is not too difficult to argue that dignity and free development require a whole flood of freedoms from this, that, or the other obstacle, right down to such ludicrous rights as freedom from failure to get a job through being unable to perform it.

The language of 'natural rights' has always been prey to this kind of criticism. For example, the Declaration of the Rights of Man and the Citizen of the French Revolution 'resolved to expound in a solemn declaration the natural, inalienable and sacred rights of man'. It maintained that in respect of their rights 'men are born and remain free and equal'. It announced that the final end of every political institution is the preservation of these rights: 'those of liberty, property, security and resistance to oppression'.

Yet these apparently harmless sentiments aroused a storm of philosophical doubt, partly fuelled by the violent anarchy of the French Revolution itself. Mainly, it is very unclear what 'a natural right' could mean. We can understand rights granted to citizens by law. We might even imagine these growing out of a very primitive society in which people afford each other something akin to rights, by habits of forbearance. Suppose A forbears from interfering with B's space, or from using violence on B, or from soliciting sexual favours from B's partner. And suppose the society would be heavily down on A were he not to forbear. Then we might talk of a convention or even a contract of forbearance, and see the beginning of a network of property rights and other social rights. B can appeal to the group to forbid or punish A's trespass, and by siding with B the others, in effect, confirm his right. But all that presupposes a society. What could exist by way of rights before or independently of a state of society? Would everyone have a right to everything? Or would nobody have a right to anything? The questions seem ludicrous.

But the language of natural rights need not be taken to raise them. It need not imply some pre-social state of nature in which, surprisingly, people nevertheless had rights of different kinds. It may be intended not as *description* of a never-never land, but as *prescription* of an order that any society should uphold. It will not then be to the point to say that the idea is unhistorical. Nor will it be to the point to say that actual society is not like this. People are not, for instance, born free—they are born into a civil order that will impose duties and obligations on them. They do not remain free in all kinds of respects, and they are not born equal and don't remain equal in all kinds of ways either. But the intention will be to criticize the existing order in the name of these ideals, or to work for an ideal that incorporates some notion of basic equality (equality before the law, for instance) and some central menu of freedoms.

Still, we might wonder about the reasons for the prescriptions. The word 'natural' in the phrase 'natural rights' might suggest a religious foundation. It would be as if God had posted on each of us at birth a small list of demands from others. If we do not find that idea appealing, then once more the word suggests some kind of Aristotelian story. Human beings will have a 'nature' that can only flourish in societies conforming to the declaration. These are the only societies in which they can 'realize' themselves or be 'truly' free. But that in turn might seem highly doubtful. We are pretty plastic and adaptive, and as we have already seen, different conceptions of flourishing abound. Many think we flourish in the rich and liberal western democracies of today. But some would say, for instance, that we can only really flourish in egalitarian societies where there are strict controls on the amount of property any one person or any one class can control. Others would say that we can only flourish under the umbrella of a strong social order, cemented by common adherence to a particular religious tradition.

We have seen that peoples' conception of their rights can be dangerously inflationary. There are other pragmatic or practical objections that have been raised. The language is abstract: how much property does a right to property give you? What duties does this right impose on others? How much does my right to life enable me to demand by way of care and resources, if those are necessary to keep me going? And we have already seen the infinitely flexible and treacherous ways in which the one-word concept of liberty can be stretched, so that a right to liberty can seem almost meaningless. One-word rights give no answer to the difficult questions.

The language is apt to be adversarial. It pits *me* against *them*, encouraging a sense of *my* right against others, *my* sense of just grievance when things don't go my way. It is not the language of genuine community; so much so that Bentham thought it was 'terrorist' language. Thus, we would not have very high expectations of a partnership in which each member is constantly checking whether his or her budget of rights has been infringed by the other. When pre-nuptial contracts specify a right to have half the washing up done, or the housework, or a right to shared child-caring duties, and sex no more than four and no less than three times a week, we should not be optimistic about the ensuing marriage. It is not that any of these things are bad—they may be desirable—but demanding them as a right implies that *me* has not been taken over by *we*. A hair-trigger sense of grievance is not a recipe for happy families. If *we* has not taken over from *me*, the attitudes needed for successful community are not in place. It is clear what Bentham would say about such a contract:

What has been the object, the perpetual and palpable object, of this declaration of pretended rights? To add as much force as possible to these passions, but already too strong—to burst the cords that hold them in,—to say to the selfish passions, there—everywhere—is your prey!—to the angry passions, there—everywhere—is your enemy. Such is the morality of this celebrated manifesto.

This was in fact the essence of Marx's later criticism of 'bourgeois' or egoistic rights. For Marx, as for many social thinkers, the notion of a 'right' is centred in a morality that is atomistic and individualistic, concentrating on the demands of the single person, and forgetting the general good of the society within which the individual is necessarily situated.

Yet for other liberal thinkers, this is exactly what is good about it (and just look at the abysmal history of communist states where the notion of individual rights had little or no place). Rights, they argue, protect us against the encroachments of the society. Even in a democracy, a minority can need protection against the tyranny of the majority. Even if insisting on rights can be egoistic, and shrill, and sometimes insensitive, still, we need the notion. We need it to describe our dependencies and our need for protection from the predations of others, including the others in their collective or political guise. Even if it is foolish to dwell on an inflated list of rights on going into a marriage, yet each partner does have rights against the other, and when they are badly infringed, redress and correction are required.

∞

PART THREE

Foundations

It is time to pick up some unfinished business. In Part I, I tried to deflect some of the hostile thoughts many people voice about ethics. But we had to acknowledge the threat of relativism, and nihilism, and scepticism. We might still fear that the voice of conscience is a delusion. We might still flounder when we try to gain some sense of its authority. Are truth and knowledge possible, or does reasoning about what to do eventually hinge on nothing but brute will? Or are there yet other alternatives?

16. REASONS AND FOUNDATIONS

Suppose we imagine an ordinary, everyday reason for acting. The everyday reason might be 'I wanted it', or 'I liked him (so I did something for him)', or 'That's what will make the most money'. A reason might be narrowly selfish, or it might be highly admirable:

'It helps to promote the greatest happiness of the greatest number' or 'It delivers people from horrendous pains and miseries'. These last two would be the reasons benevolent people offer for actions.

These reasons can be appealing. If our sympathies lie in the same direction, we will appreciate them and accept them. They work in many conversations. But there is no proof that they *have* to work. It seems to depend how much the audience sympathizes with us, or with humanity, or feels the same way as us. It seems to depend on our feelings or sentiments. And feelings or sentiments are not, on the face of it, capable of proof.

Something much grander would be a reason that everyone *must* acknowledge to be a reason, independently of their sympathies and inclinations. I shall call that a Reason, with a capital letter. It would armlock everyone. You could not ignore it or discount it just because you felt differently. It would have a necessary influence, or what philosophers sometimes call 'apodictic' force. It would bind all rational agents, insofar as they are rational. If you offer someone a reason (no capital letter) and they shrug it off, you might say they are insensitive or inhuman, callous or selfish, imprudent or senti- mental. These are defects of the heart. You may regret them, but you may not be able to prove to the audience that they are defects at all. But if you offer someone a capital-letter Reason and they shrug it off, then something different is wrong. Their very ration- ality is in jeopardy. There is something wrong with their head, if they cannot see things that just 'stand to reason'.

Philosophers, of course, are professionally wedded to reasoning, so it is natural to them to hope that we can find Reasons.

Before the eighteenth century, many moral philosophers thought that we could. They thought that fundamental principles of ethics could be seen to be true by the 'natural light of reason'. The principles had the same kind of certainty as arithmetic or geometry; you could see from your armchair that they had to be true. They were innate, or 'self-evident'. For many they were prescribed for us by a benevolent deity, so that ignoring them would be a kind of impiety. By the end of the seventeenth century, this theory had lost a lot of ground, especially among philosophers more ready to trust empirical sense experience as a source of knowledge than allegedly divine revelation. If we want provability, it began to be felt, we cannot rely on God to have put it there. But even the great empiricist John Locke (1632–1704) subscribed to a rational foundation for the basic principles of morals:

> I doubt not, but from self-evident propositions, by necessary consequences, as incontestable as those in mathematics, the measures of right and wrong might be made out, to any one that will apply himself with the same indifference and attention to the one as he does to the other of these sciences.

Locke thought this was something that could in principle be done, rather than something that had already been done. This view was swept away in the eighteenth century, first by the 'sentimentalists' the Earl of Shaftesbury (1671–1713) and Frances Hutcheson (1694–1746), but then with much greater force by David Hume, who took a dim view of the power of reason anywhere, but especially here. For Hume, reason's proper sphere is confined to mathematics and logic, while knowledge about the way things are is due solely to sense experience. Neither affords us any substantive principles of conduct. There are no Reasons. Hume drives the message home flamboyantly:

> *'Tis not contrary to reason to prefer the destruction of the whole world to the scratching of my finger. 'Tis not contrary to reason for me to choose my total ruin, to prevent the least uneasiness of an Indian or person wholly unknown to me. 'Tis as little contrary to reason to prefer even my own acknowledged lesser good to my greater.*

In other words, human reason has a limited domain. It includes mathematics and logic, for if we try to disobey their laws, thought itself becomes impossible. We are left with no ideas at all. And we can talk of the reasonable, or scientific, approach to understanding the world. But when it comes to ethics we are in the domain of preference and choice. And here, reason is silent. The heart, or what Hume called passion or sentiment, rules everything. Of course, our passions and sentiments need to operate in the world that we learn about: ignorance is a recipe for acting disastrously, both to ourselves and to others. But what the heart suggests we do, after reason and experience have found where we are, is another thing. Even basic, unambitious concerns, such as the solidarity with others or the respect for rules that were defended in sections 12 and 13, depend on sympathy. And that sympathy is not mandated by reason alone. The plight of others gives us reasons to act, certainly, but not Reasons. There may perhaps be some formal limits on our preferences: there is something 'irrational' about preferring A to B, and also at the same time preferring B to A (although it is often all right to be in two minds about things). But there are no substantive restrictions on our passions imposed by reason alone.

This could be put in terms of a contrast between *description* and *prescription*. Reason is involved in getting our descriptions of the world right. What we then prescribe is beyond its jurisdiction. Reason is in fact wholly at the service of the passions. It is just because we must act in the world that we need to know about it: 'Reason is and ought only to be the slave of the passions, and can never pretend to any other office than to serve and obey them'.

17. BEING GOOD AND LIVING WELL

As we touched upon in section 11, Aristotle thought that the *telos* or goal of a human being is to live a certain kind of life. But what kind of life? Obviously one in which certain basic biological needs for food, warmth, shelter, and perhaps sex are met (sex gets the qualification because you don't die from lacking it). Aristotle, however, managed to equate the 'intended' life for a human being with the virtuous life. He also connected it with life lived according to reason. And this may seem to give us a kind of foundation for ethics. The vicious or depraved or insensitive or callous are failing to exercise reason, the supreme human capacity.

But first of all, why think that the 'intended' or natural life for human beings is a life of virtue? On the face of it this equation requires a pretty sunny view of the human animal. We need not subscribe to a Grand Unifying Pessimism to fear that evolution has thrown up a human nature with significant elements of selfishness, aggression, shortsightedness, cruelty, and so forth. And some fairly nasty people are healthy, to judge by what the contemporary philosopher Bernard Williams nicely describes as 'the ethological standard of the bright eye and the gleaming coat'. Conversely, there may be circumstances, one would think, in which virtue requires us to sacrifice something of our own health or happiness. At the limit, virtue and duty may require us to lay down life itself. So there is no automatic alignment between behaving well and looking after ourselves.

Aristotle himself was not quite as optimistic as it might sound. He emphasized that it takes education and practice in order to become virtuous. It does not just happen, like growing taller or hairier. But the education is a matter of drawing out a 'latent' potential, at least in the best people (Aristotle is an elitist). The tradition that follows Aristotle is sometimes called the tradition of 'virtue ethics'. It heroically tries to squeeze together what is natural for people, a life lived according to reason, a happy life, and a virtuous life. Its main device is the social nature of the self. Within society, the knave or villain cannot generally flourish, either in the eyes of others, or, ultimately, in his own eyes. The life of injustice is apt to be a life of care and insecurity. If someone prospers by thieving or cheating, his prosperity is likely to turn to ashes.

Perhaps this is likely, but it is not at all certain. Still, it is good to notice that for many purposes that may be enough. A general correlation between an agent's lapse from virtue and her decline from flourishing is enough for some purposes. It is enough, for instance, for the purpose of the educator with the subject's interest at heart. The educator will not countenance a habit of finagling or lying or taking opportunistic advantage of others, since these things generally diminish the agent's well-being. We should educate people for whom we care into the habits that are most likely to benefit them, and on this account, these will be the paths of virtue. Generally speaking, people do well by doing good, or at least by avoiding doing bad.

So far so good, but it is surely a mistake to think that an equation between living as we would wish and living virtuously is somehow written into things by nature. Insofar as it is approximately true, it is because it is written into things by culture. It is in the first place an *educational* and also a *political* achievement, and one that needs constant attention. This is for at least three reasons. First, it takes education to instill into the subject the sense of respect and self-respect which will turn a profit made by selling his soul into a loss. A sufficiently barefaced villain just won't care. Second, it takes a secure and stable political or social system to generate bad effects on the villain, such as loss due to discovery, or loss of reputation. When things are in flux, the villain will be able to cheat and move on. Third, it takes a culture or politics properly to identify a lapse from virtue in any case.

To see this last point, return to our examples of oppressive societies. Suppose women systematically lack opportunities and resources that the men have. Men (and women) in such a society may not be conscious of anything wrong here. They have internalized the traditional values. Their conception of a woman flourishing will be that she is nicely subservient or obedient to the men. In such a world, the man oppressing the woman has no bad conscience, and suffers no loss of respect from those he cares about—mainly other men. He can flourish in his own eyes, and in his friends' eyes, and even in the eyes of the women. The case would be more obvious if we took behaviour towards people outside the community. We have already mentioned the tree that flourishes by depriving other trees of light, and the western white person who flourishes because of the economic and educational deprivations of people, including children, in the third world. It takes something more than a desire to flourish to motivate concern for *them*. We may measure our flourishing only amongst *ourselves* (Goya knew this).

The modern Aristotelian, less inclined to discount inferiors and outsiders than Aristotle himself, can fight back. She can say that such cases need sustaining by rationalizations, and these rationalizations will mainly consist in lies the privileged tell themselves. And we already conceded that a life lived amidst lies, or in a fool's

12. Francisco de Goya, 'As If They Are Another Breed'.

paradise, is not a flourishing life. So the ingredients are there to suggest that *real* flourishing or *true* human health implies justice. It implies removing the oppression, and living so that we can look other people, even outsiders, in the eye.

However, this need for rationalizations is itself not a given. Sometimes, as we go our careless ways, we do not even seem to need lies to sustain us. Our generation may flourish by consuming all the world's resources, and letting the future go hang. We do not tell ourselves a story according to which the generations to come are inferior to us and deserve to inherit a deadened world. We just don't think about it. It is only when we have to have a conversation with the dispossessed that we scramble for rationalizations.

Are we being 'unreasonable' as we discount or forget about dis-possessed outsiders? We are certainly failing in benevolence, and we may be failing in justice (more on this below). But even if we concede much to the Aristotelian argument, we might remain pes-simistic about its effect. Insofar as it works by 'pumping up' what is required for a life of reason or a life of *true* flourishing, we will find people perfectly ready to settle for a good fake. Better to buy the cheap running shoes and not to think too much about how they got made. To unsettle such people we will need, eventually, to look further at the motivation to justice.

18. THE CATEGORICAL IMPERATIVE

Hume's challenge to Reasons (section 16) was taken up by Im-manuel Kant. We can approach Kant's views by thinking of a common gambit in practical discussion. When we try to stop people acting in some way, a good question is often: 'What if everybody did that?' The test is sometimes called a 'universalization' test. If the answer is that something would go especially wrong if everybody did that, then we are supposed to feel badly about doing it. Perhaps, for instance, we would be claiming an exemption for ourselves that we couldn't allow to people in general.

Kant picked up the universalization test and ran with it. In his hands it became not only a particular argument *within* ethics—a device, as it were, for making people think twice, or feel guilty—but the indispensable basis *for* ethics. It became the foundation stone for ethics, grounding ethics in reason alone. It gives us Reasons, even in the domain of prescriptions or imperatives. He unveils the way this happens in his short masterpiece, the *Groundwork of the Metaphysics of Morals* of 1785, a work that has probably inspired more love and hatred, and more passionate commentary, than any other in the history of moral philosophy.

The universalization test can sound like a version of the Golden Rule: 'Do as you would be done by'—a rule sometimes claimed by Christianity as its own, but found in some form in almost every ethical tradition, including that of Confucius (551–479 BC). Kant denies that his idea is just that of the Golden Rule. It is supposed to have more meat. He points out, for example, that the Golden Rule can be misapplied. A criminal can throw it at a judge, asking him how he would like it if he were being sentenced—yet the sentence may be just, for all that. A person in good circumstances may gladly agree that others should not benefit him, if he could be excused from benefiting them. He apparently abides by the Golden Rule. So something with more structure is needed.

Kant starts by distinguishing what he wants to talk about from what he calls 'talents of the mind', such as understanding, wit, or judgement, and from advantages of temperament, such as courage or perseverance or even benevolence. He also distinguishes it from gifts of fortune, happiness, and even admirable qualities such as moderation. None of these are 'good in themselves'. For all of them can be misused, or can be lamented. Even happiness is not admirable, if it is the happiness of a villain. Benevolence may lead us astray, letting other people enjoy what they have no right to enjoy, for example. And 'the very coolness of a scoundrel makes him not only far more dangerous but also immediately more abominable in our eyes than we would have taken him to be without it'.

The only thing good in itself, then, is a good will. Even if the agent with the good will is handicapped, 'by a special disfavour of destiny or by the niggardly endowment of stepmotherly nature' from actually doing much good in the world, still, if he has a good will, it will 'shine like a jewel for its own sake'.

But what is a good will? Kant considers cases of people doing good things, things that might even be their duty, not, however, from a sense of duty, but from other inclinations, such as self-interest, or even benevolence, or a sense of vanity. A salient example is a shopkeeper who does not overcharge an inexperienced customer, but only because his self-interest is served by not doing so. Perhaps he calculates that the customer is more likely to return, or that his shop will profit from a good reputation. The shopkeeper behaves honestly enough, but not because he has the right feeling that he *ought* to do so. There is no jewel shining by itself here. This is not the good will in operation. So what is?

The shape of the answer becomes clear from such examples. The good will is one acting from a particular good motive. It is one acting out of a sense of law or duty. 'Duty is the necessity of an action from respect for law.' We are able to represent laws of action in ourselves, and a good will is one that acts in accordance with that representation. The core of morality, then, lies not in what we do, but in our motives in doing it: 'When moral worth is at issue, what counts is not actions, which one sees, but those inner principles of action that one does not see.'

This is all very well, we might say. Kant seems to be praising up the conscientious agent, or the agent of principle or righteousness or rectitude. This is a person who, once he thinks 'Such-and-such is a duty' is strong-minded or principled enough not to be deflected from doing it. This is in some respects an admirable psychology, although it is also one that can do a lot of harm, since peoples' consciences can be as perverted as anything else. One wonders why righteousness in this sense is exempt from the criticism levelled at benevolence and the rest, that it can be a Bad Thing.

Some writers also remind us that in many of life's situations, rectitude is not what we want. We often want people to act out of love or gratitude, not out of duty. Good parents take their child to an entertainment because they enjoy the child's pleasure; a parent who takes the child out of a sense of duty is to that extent lacking. A lover who kisses out of a sense of duty is due for the boot. But this is not a fundamental criticism of Kant. He can, and does, allow dimensions in which the good-hearted parent or lover or benefactor scores highly. It is just that these are not, for him, the *moral* dimensions. Moral excellence is found only in the strength of the sense of duty.

There is a more fundamental difficulty. Kant's answer seems to demand that certain things got onto a list of duties *in the first place*. It is no good saying 'Act from a sense of duty!' if when asked the question 'And what is my duty?', the only reply is 'To act from a sense of duty!'

We have to break out of the circle somewhere, and so far we do not know how. So how is it all going to get us nearer to the foundations Kant promises? His move is breathtaking, both in its speed and its result:

> But what kind of law can that be, the representation of which must determine the will, even without regard for the effect expected from it, in order for the will to be called good absolutely and without limitation? Since I have deprived the will of every impulse that could arise for it from obeying some law, nothing is left but the conformity of actions as such with universal law, which alone is to serve the will as its principle, that is, I ought never to act except in such a way that I could also will that my maxim should become a universal law.

This is the famous Categorical Imperative, or more accurately, the Categorical Imperative in its first form, the so-called Formula of Universal Law. Later on Kant glosses it in other ways. One is 'Act as if the maxim of your action were to become by your will a *universal law of nature*' (the Formula of the Law of Nature). Another, possibly the most influential, is 'So act that you use humanity, whether in your own person or in the person of any other, always at the same time as an end, never merely as a means' (the Formula of Humanity). It is not at all clear that these different versions can be derived one from the other, but Kant regarded them as somehow equivalent.

The promise is that we have here both quite substantial moral principles, or versions of the one principle, and principles that have been proved by reason alone. This last claim is hard to make good, but perhaps the idea goes like this.

As Hume illustrates, we might suppose that there are no Reasons in the area of ethics—just the desires or wills of particular persons, not necessarily shared or respected by anyone else. But Kant replies that the very formal nature of the Categorical Imperative gives it a universal authority. You cannot flout it and defend your principle in doing so. If you do flout it, you declare yourself to be un-Reasonable. If this is right, we have the required foundation: ethics comes from Reasons alone.

Unfortunately, when it comes to applications of the principle, things become a little stickier. The most persuasive examples of the Categorical Imperative doing some real work are cases where there is an institution whose existence depends on sufficient performance by a sufficient number of people. Suppose, as is plausible, that our ability to give and receive promises depends upon general compliance with the principle of keeping promises. Were we to break them sufficiently often, or were promise-breaking to become a 'law of nature', then there would be no such thing as promise-giving or promise-breaking, because no words could any longer have the required force. So, Kant considers somebody whose principle of action is, 'Let me, when hard pressed, make a promise with the intention not to keep it.' Then, says Kant, I could will the lie, but I could *not* will the universal law to lie, for in accordance with such a law there would be no promises at all. It would be willing a kind of contradiction. So we have a Reason against the lying promise.

That's all very well, but consider a person who is against the whole business of giving and receiving promises. Why shouldn't he try to undermine the institution from within: by giving false promises, with one of his aims being the breakdown of trust and cooperation? Of course, a nice or benevolent or even a prudent person wouldn't have that goal, but if Kant appeals to these virtues, the purely formal appearance of his theory begins to vanish. We only have a reason against giving the lying promise, not a Reason.

An example I like here is the institution of credit cards. These depend on enough people not paying them off each month in order to keep profits coming in to the issuing banks. So there is a kind of contradiction in imagining a world with credit cards, but where everybody pays them off each month. Suppose my principle is, 'Pay off your card whenever you feel like it.' Can I 'universalize' this, willing it to govern people in general? Surprisingly perhaps, yes. Even in a world where people can always afford to pay off their cards, we might have it that everyone pays off their card when they feel like it. This could be true provided they don't often feel like it, for instance because for most people most of the time the urge to consume is greater than the urge to save. So on the rare occasions when someone feels like paying the card off in full, she can go ahead and do so without falling foul of the Categorical Imperative. Similarly then, a person can consistently adopt principles of the kind 'Lie/break a promise/steal/cheat on taxes whenever the situation is this serious', provided the situation isn't very *often* that serious. The institutions survive, and so do the possibilities for making exceptions.

A third limitation appears if we consider the man mentioned above, who misapplies the Golden Rule, saying that he does not mind others refraining from benefiting him, provided he can be excused from benefiting them. Kant's only argument that he fails the Categorical Imperative test is that he *might* get into dire straits in which he needs the assistance of others. But this evidently invites the all-too-human rejoinder that he might not, and is willing to take the risk. He can will that nobody help anybody else, because he can gamble on staying self-sufficient.

Kant descends somewhat from the abstract heights of the Formula of Universal Law version of the Categorical Imperative. He argues in effect that the capacity of human beings to act in accordance with the imperative—the jewel within—is itself a thing of absolute, unconditional value. It is true, he thinks, that we can never be sure that we are acting from our sense of duty alone, since our motives are often mixed and often hidden from us. But at least we can set ourselves to do so. We can distance ourselves from our mundane desires and wishes, and set ourselves to act as duty requires. This capacity itself gives us our fundamental title to respect and self-respect. We are proud of our reasonings—in fact, whenever we offer reasons we are showing how much we respect reason in ourselves. So it deserves respect wherever it is found, that is, within all rational agents.

This argument (or something like it: the texts are dense) takes Kant to the Formula of Humanity: 'So act that you use humanity, whether in your own person or in the person of any other, always at the same time as an end, never merely as a means.' It is not, of course, easy to see exactly what this involves, but the general idea of remembering to respect each other is clearly attractive, and perhaps more practicable than remembering to love each other. Whether we deserve respect purely because of our capacity to make laws to ourselves is a good deal less certain. Perhaps we deserve respect from each other insofar as we are like each other in a whole mass of ways. The raiding party bent on enslaving a rival group has forgotten a shared humanity, which includes a shared capacity to love, and suffer, and hope, and fear, and remember. It hasn't *only* forgotten that the victims can reason according to general rules.

Many people think Kant offers the best possible attempt to find Reasons, and therefore to justify ethics on the basis of reason alone. Since many people want such an attempt to succeed, and fear the result if it does not, there are major intellectual industries of trying to find ever more complicated interpretations of the approach that make it work. It might be doubted whether this does much service to Kant: he was a great democrat, and believed that the necessity of the Categorical Imperative was easily visible to any reasoning creature.

19. CONTRACTS AND DISCOURSE

Some writers think that a descendant of Kant's approach, often called 'contractarianism', gives us a powerful foundation for ethics, or at least for the large part of ethics that concerns our rights and duties to each other. One formula at the centre of recent work is this, due to the contemporary American philosopher T. M. Scanlon:

> *an act is wrong if its performance under the circumstances would be disallowed by any set of principles for the general regulation of behavior that no one could reasonably reject as a basis for informed, unforced general agreement.*

As in Kant, there is a concern for the universal, and a concern for reason. A slightly different version occurs in the 'discourse ethics' of the contemporary German philosopher Jürgen Habermas. A norm of conduct has to be such that:

> *all affected can accept the consequences and the side effects its general observance can be anticipated to have for the satisfaction of everyone's interests (and the consequences are preferred to those of known alternative possibilities).*

Habermas's formulation is slightly more specific than Scanlon's. It retains a utilitarian flavour: the imagined conversation or contract is taking place between agents concerned for the satisfaction of everyone's interests. They sound to have the greatest happiness of the greatest number in their sights. By contrast, the first formula, Scanlon's version, is unspecific over what counts as 'reasonable rejection'. Suppose, for instance, we are discussing whether to organize our society on capitalist principles or more communitarian or socialist principles. Is a participant allowed to reject a proposal on the grounds that it leads to large inequalities of wealth? Or is she allowed only to voice some restricted range of reasons—such as the thought that the proposal would injure her personal interests? And in either case, are these reasons really Reasons, as Kant thought?

These questions suggest a limit to the contractarian approach. It seems that the participants in these conversations need to come with some set of values already in place. These are the things that they are prepared to offer and to accept as reasons. If the discourse were taking place between people who in advance accepted biased reasonings, then that is what would come out of the conversation. Suppose, to take the usual example, they believe that women's interests intrinsically matter less than men's, and suppose the culture has got the women to accept this. Then, of course, a set of principles coming from the 'unforced' agreement will be inegalitarian in just that respect. But then it sounds as though we need to put egalitarian ideals, ideals of liberty, or of what counts as a legitimate interest or a right, *into* the conversation at some point, in order to get them *out* at another. We also need to outlaw some other kinds of value, such as the asymmetric valuation of men and women, or a generalized phobia of people of a certain type, or a religious conception of the priority of particular ways of life. So the fear arises that the talk of discourse and contract gets short-circuited. It just disguises the real source of values, which must lie elsewhere.

The most famous proposal of this general kind in the literature is due to John Rawls, whose hugely influential book *A Theory of Justice* has dominated this branch of moral and political philosophy ever since it appeared in 1971. Rawls applies the device of a contract only to the business of finding overall principles of justice for the ordering of society. And he carefully restricts the range of considerations his contractors can advance. He imagines them having to find the overall principles from behind a 'veil of ignorance'. This means that they aren't to know which social role they might end up occupying. The idea is that if you don't know whether you will end up rich or poor, male or female, boss or worker, you will bend your mind to adopting principles of justice between each group. It is rather like cutting a cake and not knowing which bit you will end up with: a procedure that enforces a fair distribution. Rawls in fact calls his conception, 'justice as fairness'.

His contractors are also not allowed to bring specific values to the conversation. They can, however, bring care about the basic things virtually all human beings care about for themselves: safety, security of possession, the satisfaction of basic needs, a basis for self-respect. Rawls argues that what they would or should agree to, under those circumstances, is, not surprisingly, a constitution that guarantees a lot of liberties. But it is also one that regulates the economy, although subject to the protection of those liberties (you would not be allowed to trade free speech for extra wealth, for example). It regulates the economy in the interests of the least well off. It is not a free-market state, nor a purely egalitarian or communist state. It most closely resembles the democratic socialist countries of western Europe, with their substantial 'welfare floors'. However, it is more radical ('left') than them, since even after a welfare floor has been established, those least well off can make claims to further redistribution of resources. They can go on doing that until the point at which their demands damage the economy sufficiently that the whole cake diminishes, because people have insufficient incentive to work, so that the plight of the worst off becomes worse. The priority of the social and economic order, in other words, is to maximize the minimum.

However attractive some may find the Rawlsian vision of society, it is once more doubtful whether the idea of a contract is doing the work. It sounds rather as if he is describing the kind of society that certain kinds of person would prefer. These are persons who are not attached to a particular view about the good life, except that they are jealous about their liberties, and who are highly 'risk averse'. This means that they fear coming at the bottom of an unequal economic order more than they prize the rewards of an economy that allows the rich to get richer, but treats the poorest rather worse. Perhaps many of us are like that, although there are plenty of people prepared to gamble freedoms for economic advantage, or to gamble security against opportunity. Again, the apparatus of a contract seems to be short-circuited, and we are left only with the preferences and values with which we entered. They are civilized, attractive, cautious, and even quite widely shared preferences, but no more.

Yet there is something attractive as well about the image of ethics emerging from the procedures necessary to find a common point of view. The conversations we are imagining are cooperative attempts to find joint solutions to common problems. The ambition is that we can give a procedural foundation to ethics. Ethical principles are those that would be agreed upon in any reasonable cooperative procedure for coming to one mind about our conduct.

20. THE COMMON POINT OF VIEW

Usually when a great philosopher, such as Kant, overreaches himself, or seems to do so, we can suspect that there is something true in the offing. In fact, something true was already prominent among the philosophers in the generation preceding Kant.

Let us return to the business of giving and receiving reasons for action, or for attitudes in general. This is an activity that is necessary to us in society. But it is also an activity that seems to require a presupposition. The presupposition is that what I advance as a reason, a reason from my point of view, *can* be appreciated from *your* point of view. If this were not so, conversation about practical matters would seem to be reduced to one side saying 'Me, me, me', and the other side saying the same. There would then be no possibility of each side *sharing* an understanding of the situation, or coming to a *common point of view* on the factors in virtue of which something is to be done. To achieve cooperation, we need to pursue the issue jointly, to end up 'in one mind' about the solution. Hume put this by saying,

> When a man denominates another his enemy, his rival, his antagonist, his adversary, he is understood to speak the language of self-love, and to express sentiments peculiar to himself, and arising from his particular circumstances and situation. But when he bestows on any man the epithets of vicious or odious or depraved, he then speaks another language, and expresses sentiments in which, he expects, all his audience are to concur with him. He must here therefore depart from

his private and particular situation, and must choose a point
of view common to him with others.

Our practices of reasoning, then, require us to speak this 'other language'. If I expect the world to join with me in condemning someone, I cannot just say that he is my enemy. I have to engage the
passions of others by painting him as vicious or odious or depraved: hateful in general.

Fortunately we are capable of the common point of view here
described. If we are discussing which car to choose, we can expect
shared standards derived from what we want from a car: comfort,
reliability, economy, power, and so forth. If you advance a reason
for the choice that I do not share, we can go on to deploy general
standards for whether such a factor should itself count as a reason.
There is no guarantee that we will come to the same conclusion, of
course, but there is a guarantee that we *might* do so. And that is
enough to make the conversation a rational option, better than imposition of one solution on everyone, by force or violence.

If we think of ethics in this way, we may retain something from
the spirit of Kant's discussion. Suppose someone turns out to have
given us a promise that she had no intention of keeping. We may be
doubtful about Kant's ambition of showing that she was un-Reasonable, or in some kind of state akin to self-contradiction. But we
may be able to say more than just that we don't like it. We can say,
at least, that she could not expect the principle of her action to be
appreciated and agreed to, in any cooperative conversation designed to bring all parties to one mind about what she did. At least,
she could only expect us to agree if she has some story that does

gain a purchase on us, such as the absolute necessity of the promise to our own welfare, or that of others we care about. And if the agent cannot defend her principle in this kind of conversation, then even if she is not wholly un-Reasonable (with the capital letter), she *is* out of court. She has turned her back on the cooperative process of reasoning with others. She has no concern for the common point of view. We might say that she shows no respect for *our* point of view. And this is one way of being unreasonable—maybe even un-Reasonable.

We might also build on our social needs and natures here. Suppose I do an action in some circumstance for some reason. Then the whole activity of presenting my reason for acting to you implies a kind of hope that you will see my reason as having been *permissible*. I want you to acknowledge that it was all right to act like that, in that circumstance, for that reason. So long as I need that recognition, I need to seek justification from the common point of view.

We may not care about coming to one mind. *We* may exclude *them*, rationalizing our exclusion in terms of their ignorance, or their inferiority in other ways, their perverse standards, or their dreadful desires. We may want only to impose our wills, or not care whether we gain their cooperation by manipulation and deceit. So a procedural approach is quite consistent with Hume's doubts about Reason, as his own way of approaching the common point of view shows. At the back of things there lies a passion: the concern to avoid imposition and manipulation, to be able to reject the charge that *their* interests have been discounted, and to find just the common standards that enable *us* to look them in the eye.

These may be no more than concerns or passions, but they are after all the concerns and passions that enable common humanity to go forward.

The question of foundations is still open, however, for a common point of view can sometimes seem like a myth. Suppose you have a piano on your foot, which is hurting you. From your point of view your hurt dominates the situation, and gives you urgent and sufficient reason to get the piano off your foot. How can I share that point of view? I cannot myself feel your pain, or be motivated as you are by that pain. From the standpoint of those who are hurting or dispossessed it can seem like the most awful cant if we who are in comfort come along and reassure them that we share their point of view. 'I share your pain' is the sentimental drivel of the talk show.

What we can do is to take up the reasons of others and make them our own. We do not merely understand the man who gives as his reason for moving the piano that it was hurting his foot. We can also take his hurt as our motivation. His discomfort *can* become our discomfort—not in our foot, but in a desire to alter the situation for his benefit. For good people it is very uncomfortable to be in the presence of someone in pain and not be able to do anything about it. In this case, what is activating us is empathy or benevolence, not any kind of procedural rule on discourse. It is contingent how far we internalize the pains and problems of others. When they are near to us, either by ties of kinship or even just by physical proximity, we tend to be more disturbed than when they are far away. In all this we seem to have the operation of the passions, rather than the operation of Reasons. In this sense, the foundations of moral motivations are not the procedural rules on a kind of discourse, but the feelings to which we can rise. As Confucius saw long ago, benevolence or concern for humanity is the indispensable root of it all.

21. CONFIDENCE RESTORED

In Part I we considered the relativist's challenge. We may not seem to have done all that well in answering it. We have not found authoritative ethical prescriptions built into the order of things. No god wrote the laws of good behaviour into the cosmos. Nature has no concern for good or bad, right or wrong.

At our best, or so I have argued, we do have these concerns. Not all principle is hypocrisy. In any event, we cannot get behind ethics. We need standards of behaviour, in our own eyes, and we need recognition in the eyes of others. So our concern is not to 'answer' the relativist by some cunning intellectual or metaphysical trick. Our concern can only be to answer the challenge from within a set of standards which we uphold.

From within our self-understanding, we can admit that those standards are ours—just ours. We legislate them for ourselves, and also for others, when we demand respect or civility or forbearance from them. They give us reasons, not Reasons. But this understanding of what we have done does not have to be corrosive or sceptical. On the contrary, it can energize us to defend ourselves when those standards are belittled and threatened. If the self-understanding proves to be debunking, that is itself an artefact of the ethical climate of an age—in the postmodernist age, a climate of self-doubt, or loss of confidence, or cynicism, or just contempt for the enterprise of thinking about human living except in the most superficial ways.

So is there such a thing as moral knowledge? Is there moral progress? These questions are not answered by science, or religion, or metaphysics, or logic. They have to be answered from within our own moral perspective. Then, fortunately, there are countless small, unpretentious things that we know with perfect certainty. Happiness is preferable to misery, and dignity is better than humiliation. It is bad that people suffer, and worse if a culture turns a blind eye to their suffering. Death is worse than life; the attempt to find a common point of view is better than manipulative contempt for it.

The answer to the question of progress, once more, is given from within the values we can deploy. This does not mean that the answer has to be 'Yes—there is the progress that brought us to where we are!' Such triumphalism is not uncommon, but it is not logically forced upon us. We can turn our standards on themselves, and the answer does not have to be a ringing endorsement. We can fear that here and there our very own ethical atmosphere is not only imperfect, but worse than it once was. We can in principle listen to stories of a Golden Age, when things that we recognize in ourselves as faults and flaws were absent. We can admire the moral order of Confucianism, or the stress on harmony with nature in Taoism, or the resignation of the Stoics, and wonder about progress. We can cringe at the complacency of, say, nineteenth-century European thought, with its self-satisfied belief that it represented the march of progress or civilization away from the primitive or savage ways of the rest of the world. We can wonder whether contemporary obsession with rights, to the exclusion of any thought about the capacities of the people with the rights, is entirely healthy. And we can certainly be on the alert for traces of complacency in ourselves.

But if we reflect on an increased sensitivity to the environment, to sexual difference, to gender, to people different from ourselves in a whole variety of ways, we can see small, hard-won, fragile, but undeniable causes of pride. If we are careful, and mature, and imaginative, and fair, and nice, and lucky, the moral mirror in which we gaze at ourselves may not show us saints. But it need not show us monsters, either.

Appendix

THE UNITED NATIONS' UNIVERSAL DECLARATION OF HUMAN RIGHTS

Preamble

Whereas recognition of the inherent dignity and of the equal and inalienable rights of all members of the human family is the foundation of freedom, justice and peace in the world,

Whereas disregard and contempt for human rights have resulted in barbarous acts which have outraged the conscience of mankind, and the advent of a world in which human beings shall enjoy freedom of speech and belief and freedom from fear and want has been proclaimed as the highest aspiration of the common people,

Whereas it is essential, if man is not to be compelled to have recourse, as a last resort, to rebellion against tyranny and oppression, that human rights should be protected by the rule of law,

Whereas it is essential to promote the development of friendly relations between nations,

Whereas the peoples of the United Nations have in the Charter reaffirmed their faith in fundamental human rights, in the dignity and worth of the human person and in the equal rights of men and women and have determined to promote social progress and better standards of life in larger freedom,

Whereas Member States have pledged themselves to achieve, in cooperation with the United Nations, the promotion of universal respect for and observance of human rights and fundamental freedoms,

Whereas a common understanding of these rights and freedoms is of the greatest importance for the full realization of this pledge,

Now, therefore,

The General Assembly,

Proclaims this Universal Declaration of Human Rights as a common standard of achievement for all peoples and all nations, to the end that every individual and every organ of society, keeping this Declaration constantly in mind, shall strive by teaching and education to promote respect for these rights and freedoms and by progressive measures, national and international, to secure their universal and effective recognition and observance, both among the peoples of Member States themselves and among the peoples of territories under their jurisdiction.

Article 1

All human beings are born free and equal in dignity and rights. They are endowed with reason and conscience and should act towards one another in a spirit of brotherhood.

Article 2

Everyone is entitled to all the rights and freedoms set forth in this Declaration, without distinction of any kind, such as race, colour, sex, language, religion, political or other opinion, national or social origin, property, birth or other status.

Furthermore, no distinction shall be made on the basis of the political, jurisdictional or international status of the country or territory to which a person belongs, whether it be independent, trust, non-self-governing or under any other limitation of sovereignty.

Article 3

Everyone has the right to life, liberty and security of person.

Article 4

No one shall be held in slavery or servitude; slavery and the slave trade shall be prohibited in all their forms.

Article 5

No one shall be subjected to torture or to cruel, inhuman or degrading treatment or punishment.

Article 6

Everyone has the right to recognition everywhere as a person before the law.

Article 7

All are equal before the law and are entitled without any discrimination to equal protection of the law. All are entitled to equal protection against any discrimination in violation of this Declaration and against any incitement to such discrimination.

Article 8

Everyone has the right to an effective remedy by the competent national tribunals for acts violating the fundamental rights granted him by the constitution or by law.

Article 9

No one shall be subjected to arbitrary arrest, detention or exile.

Article 10

Everyone is entitled in full equality to a fair and public hearing by an independent and impartial tribunal, in the determination of his rights and obligations and of any criminal charge against him.

Article 11

Everyone charged with a penal offence has the right to be presumed innocent until proved guilty according to law in a public trial at which he has had all the guarantees necessary for his defence.

No one shall be held guilty of any penal offence on account of any act or omission which did not constitute a penal offence, under national or international law, at the time when it was committed. Nor shall a heavier penalty be imposed than the one that was applicable at the time the penal offence was committed.

Article 12

No one shall be subjected to arbitrary interference with his privacy, family, home or correspondence, nor to attacks upon his honour and reputation. Everyone has the right to the protection of the law against such interference or attacks.

Article 13

Everyone has the right to freedom of movement and residence within the borders of each State.

Everyone has the right to leave any country, including his own, and to return to his country.

Article 14

Everyone has the right to seek and to enjoy in other countries asylum from persecution.

This right may not be invoked in the case of prosecutions genuinely arising from non-political crimes or from acts contrary to the purposes and principles of the United Nations.

Article 15

Everyone has the right to a nationality.

No one shall be arbitrarily deprived of his nationality nor denied the right to change his nationality.

Article 16

Men and women of full age, without any limitation due to race, nationality or religion, have the right to marry and to found a family. They are entitled to equal rights as to marriage, during marriage and at its dissolution.

Marriage shall be entered into only with the free and full consent of the intending spouses.

The family is the natural and fundamental group unit of society and is entitled to protection by society and the State.

Article 17

Everyone has the right to own property alone as well as in association with others.

No one shall be arbitrarily deprived of his property.

Article 18

Everyone has the right to freedom of thought, conscience and religion; this right includes freedom to change his religion or belief, and freedom, either alone or in community with others and in public or private, to manifest his religion or belief in teaching, practice, worship and observance.

Article 19

Everyone has the right to freedom of opinion and expression; this right includes freedom to hold opinions without interference and to seek, receive and impart information and ideas through any media and regardless of frontiers.

Article 20

Everyone has the right to freedom of peaceful assembly and association.

No one may be compelled to belong to an association.

Article 21

Everyone has the right to take part in the government of his country, directly or through freely chosen representatives.

Everyone has the right to equal access to public service in his country.

The will of the people shall be the basis of the authority of government;

this will shall be expressed in periodic and genuine elections which shall be by universal and equal suffrage and shall be held by secret vote or by equivalent free voting procedures.

Article 22

Everyone, as a member of society, has the right to social security and is entitled to realization, through national effort and international co-operation and in accordance with the organization and resources of each State, of the economic, social and cultural rights indispensable for his dignity and the free development of his personality.

Article 23

Everyone has the right to work, to free choice of employment, to just and favourable conditions of work and to protection against unemployment.

Everyone, without any discrimination, has the right to equal pay for equal work.

Everyone who works has the right to just and favourable remuneration ensuring for himself and his family an existence worthy of human dignity, and supplemented, if necessary, by other means of social protection.

Everyone has the right to form and to join trade unions for the protection of his interests.

Article 24

Everyone has the right to rest and leisure, including reasonable limitation of working hours and periodic holidays with pay.

Article 25

Everyone has the right to a standard of living adequate for the health and well-being of himself and of his family, including food, clothing, housing and medical care and necessary social services, and the right to security in the event of unemployment, sickness, disability, widowhood, old age or other lack of livelihood in circumstances beyond his control.

Motherhood and childhood are entitled to special care and assistance. All children, whether born in or out of wedlock, shall enjoy the same social protection.

Article 26

Everyone has the right to education. Education shall be free, at least in the elementary and fundamental stages. Elementary education shall be compulsory. Technical and professional education shall be made generally available and higher education shall be equally accessible to all on the basis of merit.

Education shall be directed to the full development of the human personality and to the strengthening of respect for human rights and fundamental freedoms. It shall promote understanding, tolerance and friendship among all nations, racial or religious groups, and shall further the activities of the United Nations for the maintenance of peace.

Parents have a prior right to choose the kind of education that shall be given to their children.

Article 27

Everyone has the right freely to participate in the cultural life of the community, to enjoy the arts and to share in scientific advancement and its benefits.

Everyone has the right to the protection of the moral and material interests resulting from any scientific, literary or artistic production of which he is the author.

Article 28

Everyone is entitled to a social and international order in which the rights and freedoms set forth in this Declaration can be fully realized.

Article 29

Everyone has duties to the community in which alone the free and full development of his personality is possible.

In the exercise of his rights and freedoms, everyone shall be subject only to such limitations as are determined by law solely for the purpose of securing due recognition and respect for the rights and freedoms of others and of meeting the just requirements of morality, public order and the general welfare in a democratic society.

These rights and freedoms may in no case be exercised contrary to the purposes and principles of the United Nations.

Article 30

Nothing in this Declaration may be interpreted as implying for any State, group or person any right to engage in any activity or to perform any act aimed at the destruction of any of the rights and freedoms set forth herein.

Notes
and Further
Reading

INTRODUCTION

1 'In the eyes of some thinkers . . .' In G. W. F. Hegel, *The Phenomenology of Spirit*, the interplay mentioned here is heavily dramatized as the so-called 'master-slave' dialectic, in section B, part A, pp. 111–19. The essential point is that if you don't recognize the value of others, their recognition of your value will in turn be meaningless to you. The point is more elegantly made in Groucho Marx's 'I wouldn't want to belong to any club that would have me as a member'. A more serious treatment is Charles Taylor, *Sources of the Self*.

7 Throughout the book, when I want to highlight a thought that

separates insiders from outsiders, I use italics—it is the contrast between *us* and *them*. But I want the italic also to play something of a distancing role. For in many contexts to put the issue in terms of an 'us' and a 'them' is itself problematic. It suggests divisiveness, and it suggests that each side is somehow monolithic, thereby fudging differences within groups. We sometimes need to be sceptical about each implication.

PART I. SEVEN THREATS TO ETHICS

13 'Under Christianity the instincts . . .' Friedrich Nietzsche, *The AntiChrist*, §21. If we want a less philosophical version of the same complaint, Robert Burns's poem 'Holy Willie's Prayer' is a marvellous dissection of the low-church, Presbyterian association of holiness with servility, self-satisfaction, and vindictiveness.

17 'The blessed and immortal nature . . .' Epicurus, 'Principal Doctrines', §1, in Epicurus, *The Extant Remains*, p. 95.

20 'Everything goes to make me certain . . .' Herodotus, *The Histories*, 3. 38, p. 185.

31 'these homely methods . . .' I call these methods homely, but they are also part of the foundations of scientific method. According to Mill's authoritative account, if you want to find whether one thing is responsible for another, you try varying the circumstances, and see if you can separate them. If you can, the claim to causal responsibility fails. This is the method employed here. For more refined statements, see J. S. Mill, *A System of Logic*, bk. III, ch. 8, 'Of the Four Methods of Experimental Inquiry'.

33 'Popper asked him . . .' Karl Popper, *Conjectures and Refutations*, p. 35.

34 'Veblen noticed . . .' In fact, Veblen's view was anticipated by Adam Smith (1723–90), whose poor opinion of the motives that fuel con-

sumers is often forgotten by apostles of free markets who like to flourish his name. See *The Theory of Moral Sentiments*, I. iii. 2. 1, p. 50. The idea can also be traced back to the 'wisdom' tradition including Biblical works such as Ecclesiastes.

35 'a man who runs upon certain ruin . . .' Joseph Butler, *Fifteen Sermons*, Sermon XI, pp. 168–9.

37 Section 4 sums up a more detailed treatment given in chapter 5 of my *Ruling Passions*.

39 'The confusion strikes again . . .' A lot of political science, based on so called 'rational actor' theory, would predict that events such as tipping the restaurant staff, whom you will never meet again, wouldn't happen. It would also predict that people don't vote, since the typical cost of voting in time and effort exceeds the expectation of gain from doing so. This is because the probability of your one vote making the difference is vanishingly small. Fortunately people do not generally behave as the theory would predict.

43 Dawkins himself invented a term for ideas which, as we say, 'have a life of their own'. He calls them memes. The selfish gene/selfish person meme is a particularly virulent one, in spite of being disowned by its parent. Again, there is a longer and more detailed discussion of this in *Ruling Passions*.

44 I devote chapter 3 of *Think* to the general problems of free will and fatalism.

44 'Imagine a particularly ascetic monastic order . . .' Although, equally, a large chunk of Christian energy went into showing that sexual desire was itself voluntary, and hence a subject for guilt. See Michel Foucault, 'The Battle for Chastity', in *Essential Works of Foucault, 1954–84*, vol. I.

47 'said in a lofty, disdainful tone . . .' Immanuel Kant, 'On the Com-

mon Saying: That May Be Correct in Theory, but it is of No Use in Practice', *Practical Philosophy*, p. 280.

FURTHER READING. Doubts about ethics itself are voiced in Nietzsche, *Beyond Good and Evil*, and many other works. See also John Mackie, *Ethics: Inventing Right and Wrong*, Bernard Williams, *Ethics and the Limits of Philosophy*, and Alasdair MacIntyre, *After Virtue*. Relativism is treated in G. Harman and J. J. Thomson, *Relativism and Moral Objectivity*, and David Wong, *Moral Relativity*. The theme of multiculturalism and universal ethics is treated in many papers in *Women, Culture, and Development*, ed. Martha Nussbaum and Jonathan Glover. The demandingness of ethics is uncomfortably visible in works such as Peter Unger, *Living High and Letting Die*, and Shelly Kagan, *The Limits of Morality*. The nature of moral luck is explored in Bernard Williams, *Moral Luck*. In fiction, works such as William Golding, *The Lord of the Flies*, or A. S. Byatt, *Babeltower*, give lurid examples of moral breakdown in groups isolated from a culture.

PART II. SOME ETHICAL IDEAS

57 On missing women, see Amartya Sen, 'Women's Survival as a Development Problem', *Bulletin of the American Academy of Arts and Sciences*, 43; also 'Missing Women', *British Medical Journal*, vol. 304 (1992), p. 587.

62 'To fit in . . .' Thucydides, *History of the Peloponnesian War*, bk. 3, sect. 82, p. 242.

62 'In one of the most famous . . .' Judith Jarvis Thomson, 'A Defense of Abortion'.

65 'Death is nothing to us . . .' Epicurus, 'Principal Doctrines', II, in Epicurus, *The Extant Remains*, p. 95.

66 'Yonder all before us . . .' Andrew Marvell, 'To His Coy Mistress'.

68 'as David Hume argued ...' Hume, *Dialogues Concerning Natural Religion*, sect. x.

72 'Thou shalt not kill ...' Arthur Hugh Clough, 'The New Decalogue'.

75 'I wonder if I might call ...' P. G. Wodehouse, *The Mating Season*, p. 41; 'I doubt, as a matter of fact ...', p. 86. Marcus Aurelius was Roman Emperor from 161 to his death in 180.

76 'Vanity of vanities ...' Ecclesiastes 1: 2–3.

76 'the fine and subtle net ...' George Berkeley, *A Treatise Concerning the Principles of Human Knowledge*, introduction, sect. 20.

79 'Where I seem to differ ...' F. P. Ramsey, *The Foundations of Mathematics*, p. 291. Seventeen stone is 238 pounds or approximately 108 kilograms.

81 'useful or agreeable ...' David Hume, *An Enquiry Concerning the Principles of Morals*, IX. 1, p. 270.

81 '*eudaimonia*'. Aristotle, *Nicomachean Ethics*, 1095a.

82 'the greatest happiness ...' Although this phrase is associated with Jeremy Bentham, it was first used by Frances Hutcheson, in his *Inquiry into the Origin of our Ideas of Beauty and Virtue*, iii. 8.

82 'Mill ... argued that it is the critic ...' *Utilitarianism*, ch. 2. For Bentham on pleasure, see his *Introduction to the Principles of Morals and Legislation*, ch. 4.

91 'What governor of a town ...' David Hume, 'Of Passive Obedience', in *Essays, Moral, Political and Literary*.

96 'Augustus was sensible ...' Edward Gibbon, *Decline and Fall of the Roman Empire*, vol. I, p. 64.

100 'who shall guard the guardians?' Juvenal, *Satires*, vi. 347.

107 'What has been the object ...' Jeremy Bentham, *Anarchical Fallacies*, quoted in Waldron, *Nonsense upon Stilts*, p. 44.

FURTHER READING. On the moral problem of abortion, see *The Problem of Abortion*, ed. Susan Dwyer and Joel Feinberg. For more on the death wish, see Sigmund Freud, *Civilization and its Discontents*, and many other writings.

For attitudes to death, see Thomas Nagel, *Mortal Questions*, or Jay Rosenberg, *Thinking Clearly about Death*. For a history of the subject, see Jonathan Dollimore, *Death, Desire and Loss*. On different conceptions of happiness, see Julia Annas, *The Morality of Happiness*. The classic statement of utilitarianism is John Stuart Mill, *Utilitarianism*. For 'indirect' utilitarianism, see R. M. Hare, *Moral Thinking: Its Levels, Method, and Point*. For a fascinating history of 'natural rights' see Jeremy Waldron's *Nonsense upon Stilts: Bentham, Burke and Marx on the Rights of Man*.

PART III. FOUNDATIONS

110 'I doubt not . . .' John Locke, *An Essay Concerning Human Understanding*, IV. iii. 18, p. 549.

111 ' 'Tis not contrary . . .' David Hume, *A Treatise of Human Nature*, II. iii. 3, p. 416.

112 'Reason is and ought only to be . . .' Hume, *Treatise*, II. iii. 3, p. 415.

113 'the ethological standard . . .' Bernard Williams, *Ethics and the Limits of Philosophy*, p. 46.

118 'the very coolness of a scoundrel . . .' This and the subsequent quotations are from Immanuel Kant, *Groundwork of the Metaphysics of Morals*, p. 62

125 'an act is wrong if . . .' T. M. Scanlon, *What We Owe to Each Other*, p. 153.

129 'When a man denominates . . .' David Hume, *An Enquiry Concerning the Principles of Morals*, IX. 1, pp. 272–3

FURTHER READING. On Kant's approach to ethics, see Thomas Hill, *Dignity and Practical Reason in Kant's Moral Theory*. For Aristotelianism and virtue ethics, see Alasdair MacIntyre, *After Virtue*, or more positively, Rosalind Hursthouse, *On Virtue Ethics*. On contractarianism, see Brian Skyrms, *The Evolution of the Social Contract*, David Gauthier, *Morals by Agreement*, and T. M. Scanlon, *What We Owe to Each Other*. An excellent collection of papers on the foundations of ethics is *The Blackwell Guide to Ethical Theory*, ed. Hugh LaFollette.

Picture
Credits

The author and publisher gratefully acknowledge permission to reproduce the illustrations in this volume.

1. 'Zwei Männer, einander in hoherer Stellung vermutend, sich begenen / Two Men Meet, Each Believing the Other To Be in a Higher Position', by Paul Klee, 1903. Etching, 12 x 23 cm. Paul Klee Stiftung, Kunstmuseum Bern. © DACS 2000.

2. 'Accidental Napalm Attack, South Vietnam, 8 June 1972', photo by Hung Cong ('Nick') Ut/Associated Press.

3. 'This is the wall, Foster . . ', cartoon by Smilby, from *Punch*. © Punch Ltd.

4. 'The Human Genetic Code, Deciphered', cartoon by Matt Davies. The *Journal News/Los Angeles Times* Syndicate.

5. 'The Soul Exploring the Recesses of the Grave', by William Blake, from *The Grave: A Poem*, by Robert Blair, 1808. Reproduction by permission of the Syndics of the Fitzwilliam Museum, Cambridge.

6. 'The Just Upright Man is Laughed to Scorn', by William Blake, from *Illustrations of the Book of Job*, 1825. Reproduction by permission of the Syndics of the Fitzwilliam Museum, Cambridge.

7. 'What Is It that Makes Today's Homes so Different, so Appealing?', by Richard Hamilton, 1956. © Richard Hamilton 2000. All rights reserved DACS/Anthony d'Offay Gallery, London.

8. 'The Cockfight', by William Hogarth. © The British Museum.

9. 'Gardens of the Human Condition', cartoon by Michael Leunig, *Melbourne Age*, 8 October 1988. Michael Leunig/*The Age*.

10. 'Liberty Leading the People, 28 July 1830', by Eugène Delacroix. The Louvre, Paris. Photo © RMN/Hervé Lewandowski.

11. 'Waving the Flag', 1947–8, by George Grosz (1893–1959). Watercolour on paper. Sight: 25 x 18 in. (63.5 x 45.7 cm). Collection of Whitney Museum of American Art. Purchase and exchange, 54.9. © DACS 2000. Photo © 2000: Whitney Museum of American Art, New York.

12. 'As If They Are Another Breed', by Francisco de Goya, from *Disasters of War*, c. 1810. © The British Museum.

Bibliography

Anderson, Elizabeth. *Ethics and Economics*. Cambridge, Mass.: Harvard University Press, 1993.

Annas, Julia. *The Morality of Happiness*. New York: Oxford University Press, 1993.

Aristotle. *Nicomachean Ethics*, in *The Works of Aristotle Translated into English*, vol. 9, trans. W. D. Ross. Oxford: Oxford University Press, 1925.

Bentham, Jeremy. *An Introduction to the Principles of Morals and Legislation*. Buffalo, N.Y.: Prometheus Books, 1988.

Berkeley, George. *A Treatise Concerning the Principles of Human Knowledge*. Indianapolis: Hackett, 1987.

Blackburn, Simon. *Ruling Passions*. Oxford: Oxford University Press, 1998.

—— *Think*. Oxford: Oxford University Press, 1999.

Butler, Joseph. *Fifteen Sermons Preached at the Rolls Chapel*, ed. D. Matthews. London: Bell & Sons, 1953.

Dawkins, Richard. *The Selfish Gene*. Oxford: Oxford University Press, 1976.

Dwyer, Susan, and Feinberg, Joel, eds.. *The Problem of Abortion*. Belmont, Calif.: Wadsworth, 1997.

Dollimore, Jonathan. *Death, Desire and Loss*. London: Penguin Books, 1998.

Epicurus. *The Extant Remains*, trans. Cyril Bailey. Oxford: Oxford University Press, 1926.

Foucault, Michel. *Essential Works of Foucault, 1954–84*, vol. 1. London: Penguin Books, 2000.

Freud, Sigmund. *Civilization and its Discontents*, trans. Joan Rivers. London: Hogarth Press, 1949.

Gauthier, David. *Morals by Agreement*. Oxford: Oxford University Press, 1986.

Hare, R. M. *Moral Thinking: Its Levels, Method, and Point*. Oxford: Oxford University Press, 1981.

Harman, G. and Thomson, J. J. *Moral Relativism and Moral Objectivity*. Cambridge, Mass.: Blackwell, 1996.

Hegel, G. W. F. *The Phenomenology of Spirit*, trans. A. V. Miller. Oxford: Oxford University Press, 1967.

Herodotus. *The Histories*, trans. Robin Waterfield. Oxford: Oxford University Press, 1998.

Hill, Thomas. *Dignity and Practical Reason in Kant's Moral Theory*. Ithaca, N.Y.: Cornell University Press, 1992.

Hume, David. *Dialogues Concerning Natural Religion*. Indianapolis: Hackett, 1980.

—— *Enquiries Concerning Human Understanding and Concerning the Principles of Morals*, ed. L. A. Selby-Bigge. 3rd edn. revised by P. H. Nidditch. Oxford: Oxford University Press, 1975.

—— *Essays Moral, Political and Literary*, ed. Eugene Miller. Indianapolis: Liberty Classics, 1985.

—— *A Treatise of Human Nature*, ed. L. A. Selby-Bigge. Oxford: Oxford University Press, 1888.

Hursthouse, Rosalind. *On Virtue Ethics*. Oxford: Oxford University Press, 1999.

Kagan, Shelly. *The Limits of Morality*. Oxford: Oxford University Press, 1989.

Kant, Immanuel. *Groundwork of the Metaphysics of Morals*, trans. J. J. Paton. New York: Harper & Row, 1964.

—— *Practical Philosophy*, ed. Mary Gregor. Cambridge: Cambridge University Press, 1996.

LaFollette, Hugh, ed. *The Blackwell Guide to Ethical Theory*. Oxford: Blackwell, 2000.

Locke, John. *An Essay Concerning Human Understanding*, ed. P. H. Nidditch. Oxford: Oxford University Press, 1975.

MacIntyre, Alasdair. *After Virtue*. London: Duckworth, 1981.

Mackie, John. *Ethics: Inventing Right and Wrong*. Harmondsworth: Penguin Books, 1977.

Mill, John Stuart. *A System of Logic*. New York: Logmans, Green, 1936.

—— *Utilitarianism*, ed. John Gray. Oxford: Oxford University Press, 1991.

Nagel, Thomas. *Mortal Questions*. New York: Cambridge University Press, 1979.

Nietzsche, Friedrich. *Basic Writings*, trans. Walter Kaufmann. New York: Random House, 1967.

Nussbaum, Martha and Glover, Jonathan, eds. *Women, Culture, and Development*. New York: Oxford University Press, 1995.

Plato. *Euthyphro* and *Republic*, in *The Collected Dialogues*, ed. Edith

Hamilton and Huntington Cairns. Princeton, N.J.: Princeton University Press, 1961.

Popper, Karl. *Conjectures and Refutations*. London: Routledge & Kegan Paul, 1965.

Ramsey, F. P. *The Foundations of Mathematics*. London: Routledge & Kegan Paul, 1931.

Rawls, John. *A Theory of Justice*. Cambridge, Mass.: Harvard University Press, 1971.

Rosenberg, Jay. *Thinking Clearly about Death*. Indianapolis: Hackett, 1998.

Scanlon, T. M. *What We Owe to Each Other*. Cambridge, Mass.: Harvard University Press, 1998.

Sen, Amartya. 'Missing Women', *British Medical Journal*, vol. 304 (1992), p. 587.

—— 'Women's Survival as a Development Problem', *Bulletin of the American Academy of Arts and Sciences*, vol. 43.

Singer, Peter. *Practical Ethics*. Cambridge: Cambridge University Press, 1993.

Skyrms, Brian. *The Evolution of the Social Contract*. New York: Cambridge University Press, 1996.

Smith, Adam. *The Theory of Moral Sentiments*, ed. D. D. Raphael and A. L. Macfie. Oxford: Oxford University Press, 1976.

Stoppard, Tom. *Jumpers*. London: Faber & Faber, 1972.

Taylor, Charles. *Sources of the Self*. Cambridge, Mass.: Harvard University Press, 1989.

Thomson, Judith Jarvis. 'A Defense of Abortion', *Philosophy and Public Affairs*, vol. 1 (1971), pp. 47–66; reprinted in *The Problem of Abortion*, ed. Susan Dwyer and Joel Feinberg. Belmont, Calif.: Wadsworth, 1997.

Thucydides. *History of the Peloponnesian War*, trans. Rex Warner. London: Penguin Books, 1954.

Unger, Peter. *Living High and Letting Die*. New York: Oxford University Press, 1996.

Veblen, Thorstein. *The Theory of the Leisure Class*. Harmondsworth: Penguin Books, 1994.

Waldron, Jeremy. *Nonsense upon Stilts: Bentham, Burke and Marx on the Rights of Man*. London: Methuen, 1987.

Williams, Bernard. *Ethics and the Limits of Philosophy*. London: Fontana, 1985.

—— *Moral Luck*. Cambridge: Cambridge University Press, 1981.

Wodehouse, P. G. *The Mating Season*. Harmondsworth: Penguin Books, 1961.

Wong, David. *Moral Relativity*. Berkeley: University of California Press, 1984.

Index